Inference

MANUFACTURED WITH
100% WIND ENERGY

A STRATEGIC TEACHER PLC GUIDE

Inference

Teaching Students to Develop Hypotheses, Evaluate Evidence, and Draw Logical Conclusions

Harvey F. Silver | R. Thomas Dewing | Matthew J. Perini

Alexandria, Virginia USA

A GUIDE FOR PROFESSIONAL LEARNING COMMUNITIES

1703 N. Beauregard St. · Alexandria, VA 22311-1714 USA
Phone: 800-933-2723 or 703-578-9600 · Fax: 703-575-5400
Web site: www.ascd.org · E-mail: member@ascd.org
Author guidelines: www.ascd.org/write

Gene R. Carter, *Executive Director*; Judy Zimny, *Chief Program Development Officer*; Gayle Owens, *Managing Director, Content Acquisitions and Development*; Scott Willis, *Director, Book Acquisitions & Development*; Genny Ostertag, *Acquisitions Editor*; Julie Houtz, *Director, Book Editing & Production*; Miriam Goldstein, *Editor*; Georgia Park, *Senior Graphic Designer*; Mike Kalyan, *Production Manager*; Keith Demmons, *Typesetter*; Kyle Steichen, *Production Specialist*

Printed in the United States of America. Cover art © 2012 by ASCD. ASCD publications present a variety of viewpoints. The views expressed or implied in this book should not be interpreted as official positions of the Association.

All web links in this book are correct as of the publication date below but may have become inactive or otherwise modified since that time. If you notice a deactivated or changed link, please e-mail books@ascd.org with the words "Link Update" in the subject line. In your message, please specify the web link, the book title, and the page number on which the link appears.

PAPERBACK ISBN: 978-1-4166-1442-5   ASCD product #112027   n04/12

Quantity discounts for the paperback edition only: 10–49 copies, 10%; 50+ copies, 15%; for 1,000 or more copies, call 800-933-2723, ext. 5634, or 703-575-5634. For desk copies: member@ascd.org.

Library of Congress Cataloging-in-Publication Data
Silver, Harvey F.
  Inference : teaching students to develop hypotheses, evaluate evidence, and draw logical conclusions : a strategic teacher PLC guide / Harvey F. Silver, R. Thomas Dewing, and Matthew J. Perini.
      p. cm. – (A strategic teacher PLC guide)
  Includes bibliographical references.
  ISBN 978-1-4166-1442-5 (pbk. : alk. paper)
  1. Thought and thinking—Study and teaching. 2. Inference—Study and teaching. 3. Induction (Logic)—Study and teaching. I. Dewing, R. Thomas. II. Perini, Matthew J., 1973– III. Title.
  LB1590.3.S49 2012
  370.15'24–dc23
                    2012001287

20 19 18 17 16 15 14 13 12   1 2 3 4 5 6 7 8 9 10 11 12

It is difficult to imagine this work having taken shape without the wisdom of our dear and deeply missed friend, Richard Strong. Richard's brilliant work in helping schools become better and more thoughtful places will continue to inspire us.

Inference

Teaching Students to Develop Hypotheses, Evaluate Evidence, and Draw Logical Conclusions

Acknowledgments

Research Team

Joyce Wagers Jackson

Susan C. Morris

Daniel R. Moirao

Victor Klein

Barb Heinzman

The work of these Thoughtful Classroom trainers and coaches in schools across the country played a critical role in the development of the Strategic Teacher PLC Guides. The feedback the team brought back from teachers, teacher leaders, and administrators made each successive version—and there were many versions—more powerful and more practical for educators.

Special thanks go to the Green River Regional Educational Cooperative (GRREC) in Kentucky, where earlier versions of these Strategic Teacher PLC Guides were piloted with more than 100 schools. It was the vision of teacher leadership shared by Liz Storey, Jamie Spugnardi, and hundreds of other teacher leaders and administrators from GRREC schools that helped us realize the potential of this new approach to building professional learning communities in schools.

To the wonderful staff at ASCD, thank you for your support and enthusiasm for these Strategic Teacher PLC Guides.

Finally, for never letting us—or our schools—forget the central role that thought plays in every act of teaching and learning, we would like to thank Art Costa and Bena Kallick. We are proud to integrate your work in building students' habits of mind into this Strategic Teacher PLC Guide.

Introduction

About This Strategic Teacher PLC Guide

You're holding an innovative professional development tool called a Strategic Teacher PLC Guide. Designed in partnership with more than 75 schools, Strategic Teacher PLC Guides make the important work of bringing high-impact, research-based instructional practices into every classroom easier than ever before. Each guide serves as a complete professional development resource for a team of teachers (or professional learning community) to learn, plan, and implement the research-based practice in their classrooms.

This Strategic Teacher PLC Guide focuses on inference, or the ability to examine information, generate hypotheses, and draw conclusions that are not explicitly stated. Teaching students how to make inferences is more critical than ever for success in life and in school. Inference has been identified as a "foundational process" that underlies higher-order thinking and 21st century skills (Marzano, 2010). In fact, the very first College and Career Readiness anchor standard for Reading in the Common Core asks students to "Read closely to determine what the text says explicitly and to make logical inferences from it; cite specific textual evidence when writing or speaking to support conclusions drawn from the text."

This PLC Guide walks readers through four research-based, classroom-tested strategies that help develop students' inferential thinking skills:

- **Inductive Learning** helps students draw inferences by grouping data, labeling the data groups with descriptive titles, and using the groups to generate and test hypotheses.
- **Mystery** presents students with a puzzling question or situation and has students examine clues that help them explain the mystery.
- **Main Idea** teaches students how to use inferential thinking to construct main ideas that are not explicitly stated.
- **Investigation** challenges students to use various problem-solving approaches that require inference.

Inference also integrates the habits of mind, a set of dispositions that increase students' capacity for skillful thinking (Costa & Kallick, 2008, 2009).

Turning Knowledge into Practice

Here are three things we know about improving teaching and learning:

1. High-quality instruction leads invariably to higher levels of student achievement. Most educational researchers have concluded that the quality of classroom instruction is the single greatest determinant of student success.

2. High-quality instruction is replicable. There are specific, research-based strategies that are proven to raise student achievement—and they are strategies all teachers can master with time and support.

3. Schools that function as effective professional learning communities see "big, often immediate, dividends in student learning and professional morale in virtually any setting" (Schmoker, 2005, p. xii).

In other words, we know that we need to focus on improving instruction, we know which strategies will work, and we know that professional learning communities are key to any such efforts. But knowing these statements to be true doesn't mean that change is easy. In fact, we have worked with thousands of teachers and administrators who have built professional development around research-based strategies and professional learning communities, only to be disappointed by the results. Why? They were focused on the right things. They understood the crucial importance of collegial learning. What they needed was the *how. How do we make our professional learning communities work?*

The solution we developed with these schools is *learning clubs*. If you've been struggling to make the professional learning community concept a reality in your school, or if you're just beginning the process of establishing a professional learning community, learning clubs can help. A learning club is a collaborative support structure that makes the process of establishing and sustaining a professional learning community more manageable for teachers, administrators, and schools. A typical learning club consists of four to eight teachers who meet regularly to talk about and refine their instructional practices.

Learning Clubs and Strategic Teacher PLC Guides: Perfect Together

Over the years, we have found that the members of the most successful learning clubs follow a relatively standard set of guidelines to maximize the power of collaborative learning. In response, we designed the Strategic Teacher PLC Guides around these guidelines. The members of successful learning clubs

- *Concentrate on instructional techniques proven to make a difference.* That's why each Strategic Teacher PLC Guide focuses on a specific strategy backed by both research and classroom practice.
- *Learn new strategies interdependently.* That's why each Strategic Teacher PLC Guide has been designed for use by a team of teachers. Discussion, group reflection, and group processing activities are all built into its structure.
- *Use new strategies in their classrooms.* That's why each Strategic Teacher PLC Guide puts such a high premium on classroom application. Teachers plan lessons, implement them in the classroom, and evaluate the results together.
- *Bring student work back to their learning clubs.* That's why each Strategic Teacher PLC Guide includes one full section dedicated to the analysis of student work.
- *Self-assess throughout the process.* That's why each Strategic Teacher PLC Guide includes strategy implementation milestones that teachers can use to determine where they are and where they need to go next.

But Where Will We Find the Time?

As the research of Bruce Joyce and Beverly Showers (2002) makes clear, learning a new strategy is never as simple as attending a workshop or reading a chapter in a book. If you expect to implement a new strategy successfully in the classroom, then you'll need to commit at least 10–12 hours of embedded professional development time to master that strategy. Here's how some of the schools we work with address the challenge of time:

- Some schools convert their staff meetings, grade-level meetings, or department meetings into learning club sessions.
- Some schools use a portion of their committed professional development days for learning clubs.
- Some schools create intensive summer sessions for their learning clubs.
- Some schools have made a full commitment to the power of job-embedded learning and set aside regular time for learning clubs to meet on a weekly, biweekly, or monthly basis.

Because each school has unique scheduling demands and professional development resources, Strategic Teacher PLC Guides allow maximum flexibility. This guide, for example, is divided into four separate sections:

- Section 1 serves as an introductory workshop or tutorial on inference. Between Sections 1 and 2, teachers look for opportunities to incorporate inference-based activities into their instruction.
- Section 2 shows teachers how to plan and implement inference lessons in their classrooms. Between Sections 2 and 3, teachers implement their lessons in the classroom and work with a critical friend to provide reciprocal feedback on their lessons.
- In Section 3, teachers reflect on how their lessons worked in the classroom. Between Sections 3 and 4, teachers design and implement a new lesson and collect samples of student work.
- Section 4 models a process for analyzing student work and shows teachers how to use this student work to improve instructional decision making.

We recommend that you preview these four sections and develop a schedule that works for all the members of your learning club. *As a final note, make sure you photocopy the lesson planning forms before filling them out (see pp. 67–71). You will need more blank forms as you plan future lessons.*

Good luck and good learning!

Why Inference?

This section serves as an introductory tutorial on four inference strategies: Inductive Learning, Mystery, Main Idea, and Investigation. In this section, our goal is to help you reflect on your current approach to building students' inference skills in your classroom and to explain the Strategic Teacher approach to teaching inference.

In this section you will

- Draw on your past experiences with inference strategies.

- Explore the research, principles, and classroom phases behind four inference strategies.

- Examine a range of classroom applications that demonstrate the different ways inference can be used to deepen student thinking.

- Experience a model lesson using the Inductive Learning strategy.

Let's Get Started

Imagine this: you're driving on the freeway in moderate traffic when, in your rearview mirror, you suddenly see a vehicle enter the freeway at high speed. It's a huge red SUV, and it's moving quickly from lane to lane, cutting off vehicles left and right. You, being the defensive driver that you are, know reckless driving when you see it and decide to move to the right lane and allow the SUV to pass. The SUV barrels past you, and you breathe a sigh of relief.

You may or may not be the kind of defensive driver described in this scenario, but we'll give you the benefit of the doubt and assume you are. Part of what makes you a good driver is your ability to *infer*. Inference is what thinking adds to what we know, read, or learn. Speaking scientifically, we might say that inferential thinking always involves gathering information, developing hypotheses, and drawing conclusions. Applied to our driving example, inference is at work as you, the driver, take in data (there's an SUV behind me moving erratically); make an assumption or a hypothesis based on that data (that SUV is going to hit me if I stay in this lane); test your hypothesis (let's see what happens if I move into the right lane); examine the results to confirm or refute your hypothesis (the SUV didn't hit me, so it looks like I made the right choice); and learn from the process (if that happens again, I'll be sure to do the same thing).

As you can see, inference is a perfectly ordinary human capacity. But that doesn't mean it's easy for students to make inferences in school. In fact, many teachers identify inference as one of the most challenging of all academic skills to teach. They note that inference feels abstract and difficult to model, design lessons around, and assess. But teach inference we must, because inference is a "foundational skill"—a prerequisite for higher-order thinking and 21st century skills (Marzano, 2010). That's why inference and evidence gathering are both so prominent throughout the Common Core State Standards.

So what does inference look like in the classroom? What kinds of inferential thinking are required for success in school and beyond? Figure 1.1 includes some examples of typical classroom situations that require students to make inferences. Review the examples and respond to the questions that follow on page 5.

Figure 1.1 Examples of Inference in the Classroom

Overheard in Science Class

All right, we've been studying sound for almost a week now. Let's see if you can figure this one out: Since we obviously can't see around corners, why is it that we can hear around corners? How would you design a simple experiment to test your ideas?

Inference and Emily Dickinson

Think about the poet's attitude toward faith. Then explain the central message of this poem in one sentence.

"Faith" is a fine invention
When Gentlemen can *see*—
But *Microscopes* are prudent
In an Emergency.
—Emily Dickinson (c. 1860)

What's Iridium Got to Do with It?

Here's a strange question: What does the element iridium have to do with the extinction of the dinosaurs? Here are some clues to help you figure it out:

- Iridium is an element that is rare on Earth.
- High concentrations of iridium have been found in Italy, Montana, and Mexico.
- Iridium is common in objects from outer space, such as meteors and asteroids.
- In the 1980s, scientists discovered a thin layer of sediment within the Earth's crust called the K-T boundary. The K-T boundary is found worldwide, and it is rich in iridium.
- Nearly all dinosaur fossils are found below the K-T boundary.

What tentative hypotheses can you generate? Let's look at some more clues to test your hypotheses.

Figure 1.1 Examples of Inference in the Classroom (*continued*)

Introducing Fractions

So far, we've learned some key vocabulary terms, and we've looked at lots of different fractions to see how we could group them. After some heated discussion, we finally agreed on these groups and labels:

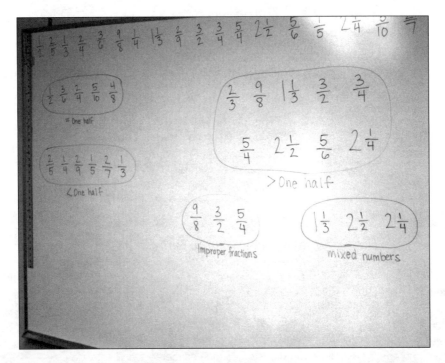

What do our groupings tell us? Before we go further, I want each of you to try to draw three conclusions about fractions. As we learn more about fractions, you'll be collecting evidence that either helps you prove your conclusions or tells you that you might need to rethink some of your conclusions.

The Mystery of the American Revolution

In your envelopes, you'll find 25 facts and images pertaining to the American Revolution. Your job is to develop a compelling answer to this question: How did a ragtag militia of untrained soldiers defeat the most powerful army in the world?

[Note that a sample set of visual clues includes British redcoats marching in crisp formation wearing bright red and white uniforms versus colonial militia in plain, brownish clothing hiding among trees and bushes.]

Activity: Thinking About Classroom Inference

What do these examples have in common?

How do students need to think to succeed in these situations?

What are some situations in your classroom that require students to think inferentially?

How do your lessons build students' inference skills?

Inference: A Family of Strategies

To help students develop the thinking skills needed to succeed on tasks like these, teachers need inference strategies. All inference strategies work in the same way: they present students with a puzzling question, a discrepant event, incomplete data, or an interesting problem to solve. Students are expected to use their powers of reasoning to develop hypotheses and then test and refine them—a skill that a wide range of researchers have found to have a significant influence on student achievement. (For a full discussion of the research and theory behind generating and testing hypotheses, see Marzano, 2007.)

What makes each inference strategy different from the others is the process students use to draw their conclusions. In this guide, we examine four inference strategies:

- **Inductive Learning**, which helps students draw inferences by grouping data, labeling the data groups with descriptive titles, and using the groups to generate and test hypotheses.
- **Mystery**, which presents students with a puzzling question or situation and has students examine clues that help them explain the mystery.
- **Main Idea**, which teaches students how to use inferential thinking to construct main ideas that are not explicitly stated.
- **Investigation**, which challenges students to use various problem-solving approaches that require inference.

As you learn about each strategy, ask yourself, How does this deepen students' interaction with the content? How does it develop students' inference skills? After reviewing all four strategies, discuss them with your learning club. What effects might these strategies have on student thinking and classroom discussion? Which would work best in your classroom? Record your thoughts in the space provided on page 14.

Inductive Learning

In Inductive Learning (based on the work of Hilda Taba, 1971), students group and label specific "bits" of information—often words—and then use the groups to generate hypotheses. For example, Figure 1.2 shows how an Inductive Learning lesson on Ancient Egypt might work.

Figure 1.2 Sample Inductive Learning Lesson: Ancient Egypt

1. Students start with a list of words related to Ancient Egypt:

moon	surgery	Ra (sun god)	high priests
scalpel	stars	planets	patients
Geb (earth god)	worship	constellations	Nut (sky god)
Kushta (medicine plant)			

2. They convert these terms into labeled groups:

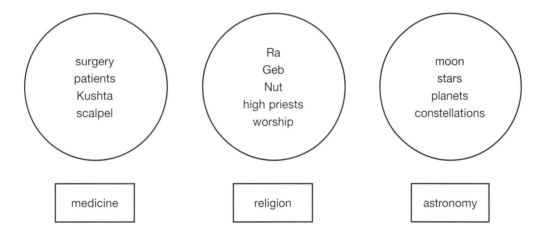

surgery
patients
Kushta
scalpel

Ra
Geb
Nut
high priests
worship

moon
stars
planets
constellations

medicine   religion   astronomy

3. They use these groups to make predictions, including the following:

- The Egyptians practiced medicine.
- Religion was very important to the Egyptians, who believed in many gods.
- The Egyptians were interested in astronomy.

4. Finally, students test and refine their predictions as they learn more about Ancient Egypt, either through a reading or during the course of a lesson or unit.

How does Inductive Learning deepen student interaction with the content?

How does Inductive Learning develop students' inference skills?

Mystery

Mystery lessons capitalize on our affinity for the puzzling and the unknown by presenting students with just enough content that they ask, "Yes, but why?" or "Yes, but how?" Students analyze clues, statements, or excerpts from primary documents to solve the mystery. For example, students might be presented with this mystery:

> We all know the old saying "In 1492, Columbus sailed the ocean blue." But why 1492? Why was the time right for Columbus's famous journey?

To solve the mystery, students would analyze a set of 20–25 clues and sort them into thematic groups. For example, Figure 1.3 depicts a set of clues about innovations in technology made during Columbus's time.

Figure 1.3 Technology Clues

New ships called caravels were faster and easier to navigate than any ship before.

_____

Inventions like the astrolabe and the mariner's compass made longer, more difficult trips possible.

_____

Cartography, or mapmaking, became more sophisticated and increasingly accurate by Columbus's time.

After sorting all the clues, students would use their clue groups to develop a compelling explanation for the mystery.

Activity: Thinking About Mystery

How does Mystery deepen student interaction with the content?

How does Mystery develop students' inference skills?

Main Idea

Teachers at all grade levels recognize that many students struggle when asked to identify the main idea of a text. Teachers know why, too: main ideas are often unstated. Instead of being able to pull a ready-made main idea out of a reading, students more typically need to construct the main idea through inference. Yet despite this knowledge, teachers often fail to teach students how to assemble details in support of a main idea.

Main Idea is a strategy that teaches students a replicable process for using inference to construct and test a main idea. Specifically, the strategy teaches students

1. How to collect "feel-important" words and phrases as they read.
2. The difference between the *topic* (the subject of the reading) and the *main idea* (a sentence that summarizes what the reading says about the topic).
3. How to test the strength of their main idea by collecting details that support it.
4. How to use a visual organizer to make notes that are accurate, organized, and easy to understand.

Figure 1.4 shows how one student used the Main Idea strategy and organizer to identify the main idea of a reading about the prehistoric "Super-Croc."

Figure 1.4 Student's Super-Croc Organizer

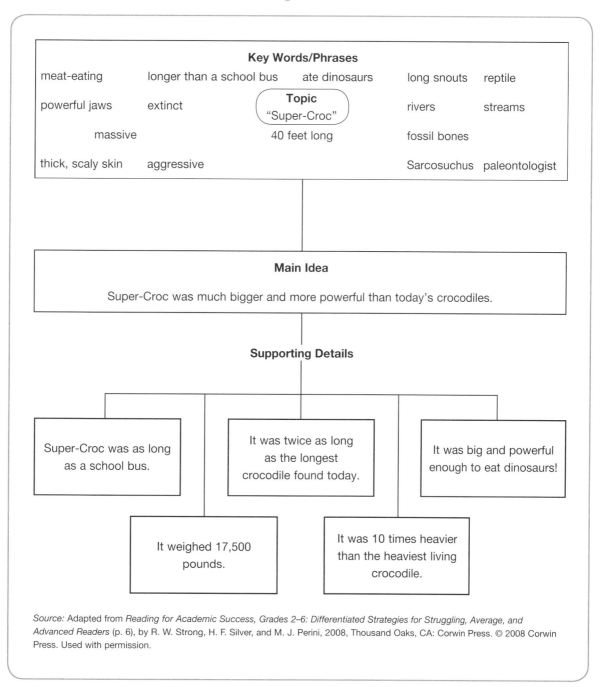

Key Words/Phrases

meat-eating   longer than a school bus   ate dinosaurs   long snouts   reptile

powerful jaws   extinct   **Topic** "Super-Croc"   rivers   streams

massive   40 feet long   fossil bones

thick, scaly skin   aggressive   Sarcosuchus   paleontologist

Main Idea

Super-Croc was much bigger and more powerful than today's crocodiles.

Supporting Details

Super-Croc was as long as a school bus.

It was twice as long as the longest crocodile found today.

It was big and powerful enough to eat dinosaurs!

It weighed 17,500 pounds.

It was 10 times heavier than the heaviest living crocodile.

Source: Adapted from *Reading for Academic Success, Grades 2–6: Differentiated Strategies for Struggling, Average, and Advanced Readers* (p. 6), by R. W. Strong, H. F. Silver, and M. J. Perini, 2008, Thousand Oaks, CA: Corwin Press. © 2008 Corwin Press. Used with permission.

How does Main Idea deepen student interaction with content?

How does Main Idea develop students' inference skills?

Investigation

Investigation lessons tend to be the most open-ended of the family of inference strategies and can be used to meet a variety of objectives or content demands. For example, you could ask students to

- **Invent or design.** "The local zoo has hired you to redesign the enclosure for an animal of your choice. The new enclosure should promote the health and happiness of your animal while providing maximum visibility and entertainment for zoo visitors."
- **Make decisions.** "Historians often argue about Lincoln's motivations as president. Some claim that Lincoln was driven by his morals and that he wanted to end slavery at any cost. Others claim that Lincoln was, above all, a pragmatist whose lone goal was preserving the Union. What do you think? Was the abolition of slavery or the preservation of the Union the driving force in Lincoln's presidency?"
- **Analyze systems or text structures.** "Let's use what we've learned about Poe's theory of the well-made tale to take a closer look at how horror stories work. Choose one horror story from our unit. Identify its parts, the purpose of each part, and how the parts work together to create a 'unity of effect.' What are the strengths and weaknesses of your chosen story? If you were the author, how would you increase its unity of effect?"

- **Experiment with a variety of problem-solving approaches.** "Today, we're going to use paper airplanes to learn about the physics of flight and air resistance. In groups of four, create and test three different airplane designs. Keep track of how adjustments in shape, paper thickness, and number of folds affect the performance of each airplane. Afterward, each group will use its findings to create a 'perfect' paper airplane to compete against the other groups' designs."

- **Speculate and make informed predictions.** "What if Thomas Edison had never lived? How might your life be different today?"

Activity: Thinking About Investigation

How does Investigation deepen student interaction with content?

How does Investigation develop students' inference skills?

Now that you've learned about the four inference strategies in this guide, discuss them with your learning club. Use the questions below to guide your discussion.

Activity: Reflecting on the Inference Strategies

1. Which strategy or strategies caught your attention?

2. Which strategy would work best in your classroom? Why do you think so?

3. How would you use the strategy?

What Can Inference Strategies Do for You and Your Students?

Teachers can use inference strategies to meet at least five important instructional goals.

GOAL #1:   **Engage Student Curiosity**

Curiosity is a powerful drive. Because inference strategies are typically built around missing information or confusing situations, they naturally raise curiosity. With a well-designed inference strategy like Mystery, the lesson becomes students' quest to figure out what's happening.

GOAL #2:   **Find Main Ideas**

By providing students with data, clues, and bits of information, inference strategies emphasize the separation of essential information from the nonessential. More specifically, the Main Idea strategy teaches students how to use the inferential process to organize relevant details and to construct and test the strength of main ideas—a crucial skill highlighted in the Common Core State Standards.

GOAL #3:   **Develop and Test Hypotheses**

The meta-analytic research of Robert Marzano (2007) shows that teaching students how to form and test hypotheses is one of the surest ways to raise achievement. Inference strategies like Mystery, Inductive Learning, and Investigation challenge students to sort through data and to turn their initial ideas into clear hypotheses. Then, in a process of continual refinement, students analyze the data more deeply to find relevant evidence that supports the validity of their hypotheses.

GOAL #4:   **Develop Powerful Explanations and Interpretations**

After students have tested their hypotheses, they must turn their findings into clear explanations or compelling interpretations that answer questions like "What's going on here? How do you know?" and "What examples, details, clues, or proofs can you offer to support your ideas?" For this reason, inference strategies are ideal for addressing the Common Core State Standards that require students to gather and use evidence.

GOAL #5:   **Develop Students' Habits of Mind**

In their years of research into the defining characteristics of intelligent behavior and thought, Art Costa and Bena Kallick (2008, 2009) have identified 16 "habits of mind." By nourishing these habits in our students, we give them the tools they need to use their minds well, thus increasing their chance for future success. Using inference strategies in the classroom will help students develop these habits of mind: thinking flexibly; thinking about thinking (metacognition); applying past knowledge to new situations; and thinking and communicating with clarity and precision.

Answer the question below, and then discuss your response with your learning club. Are there any goals that seem to be especially important to all the members of your learning club?

Activity: The Most Important Goal

Which of the five goals of inference is most important to you, and why?

The Principles and Phases of Thoughtful Inference Lessons

How do we know when students are making good inferences? Compare the two essays in Figures 1.5 and 1.6, which were written by two middle school students after completing a lesson on the colony at Jamestown. What do you notice? Discuss your ideas with a partner, focusing on the skill of inference rather than on the quality of writing. Which inferences was Clea able to make that seem to have eluded Jacob? What specific skills were evident in Clea's essay? Why do you think some students encounter difficulties or develop bad habits that cause them to flounder when asked to think inferentially? Use the space following Figures 1.5 and 1.6 to make some notes.

Figure 1.5 Clea's Essay

The Mystery of Jamestown's Vanishing Population

In the Jamestown colony in Virginia, death was everywhere. Between 1607 and 1622, an astounding 80 percent of the original population disappeared. Why was it so hard to survive in Jamestown? Because in Jamestown, profits were more important than people.

The economy of Jamestown was focused entirely on tobacco. From 1613 to 1618, tobacco exports increased from 200 to over 49,000 pounds per year, which shows how focused people were on making a profit on this crop. Tobacco was a difficult crop to harvest and it took up most of the workers' time. The corn crops became so neglected that the government instituted a law in 1618 insisting that each man plant corn or he would be strongly fined. The law got stricter each year.

Because the colonists were so focused on growing tobacco, the Jamestown colony fell apart. Nearly every square inch of land was being used for planting tobacco. People spent most of their time working on the tobacco crops. Virginia was an extremely unhealthy place to live. People were getting typhoid fever from contaminated wells, animals were disappearing, and houses were not maintained. Even the churches were used for tobacco storage. Finally, Virginia became ungovernable and crime worsened.

So why did people keep coming to Jamestown? Well, the people who came from England when conditions were already bad in Jamestown were described in an excerpt from an old newspaper as "slum dwellers, convicts, and poor farmers." They must have been very desperate people who had very little chance of succeeding in England. For those who were desperate, the idea of getting rich by growing tobacco must have been so powerful that they were willing to risk their lives by coming to one of the most dangerous places imaginable. For the poor, as well as for almost everyone else in Jamestown, the chance to make a profit came first.

Figure 1.6 Jacob's Essay

Jamestown

Life in Jamestown was tough. People were dying left and right. Everyone was so busy trying to make tobacco. They forgot to do all of the other things. They even forgot to make food like corn.

The reason was tobacco. It took too much work to grow it. But the colonists kept trying anyway. One clue said it was worth even more money than gold. Nowadays tobacco is expensive, but it's not worth as much as gold.

Activity: Notes on Students' Inference Skills

We want all of our students to be able to make inferences as well as Clea—to be able to pick out important information, make logical connections between bits of information, formulate strong hypotheses, and explain their hypotheses and conclusions thoughtfully. To help us achieve these goals, let's turn our attention to the five principles of making effective inferences. Each of the inference strategies in this guide is based on these five research-based principles, which are designed to help students develop stronger habits of mind when they collect information, make claims and hypotheses, weigh evidence, and explain what they are learning. You'll notice that these five *principles* are closely aligned with the five classroom *phases* that drive inference lessons. Leading your students through these five phases is essential for ensuring students' effective use of the strategy in the classroom. Notice that combining the first letter of each phase spells out the acronym INFER. A classroom poster highlighting the role that students play during an inference lesson is included with this guide. Figure 1.7 (p. 20) shows the five principles and corresponding phases that guide well-designed inference lessons.

Figure 1.7 The Five Principles and Classroom Phases of Inference Lessons

Principle One: What's Missing Is What's Important
 	
All inference strategies are built on partial or missing information, whether it's a main idea to be constructed or the solution to be discovered. It is the students' job to use their reasoning and inference skills to fill in the gaps.
	Phase One: *I*dentify What You Need to Figure Out
	
	• Pique students' interest with a thought-provoking hook.
	• Explain to students
	    – What they're looking for.
	    – The strategy they'll be using.
	    – Their role in the lesson.

Principle Two: Understanding Is a Drive The human mind hates being in the dark; we all have a drive to understand—to find the patterns, put pieces together, and make sense of our surroundings. To capitalize on this drive, inference strategies treat information sources as clues that students use to help them make discoveries. Thoughtful inference strategies also include visual organizers that help students see the patterns and relationships within the information.	**Phase Two: *N*ote Information Sources and Look for Patterns** • Provide students with (or help them find or generate) the resources they need to figure out what's missing. • Reinforce the idea that information sources offer clues. • Provide students with a visual organizer that helps them see patterns, and model its use.
Principle Three: Inference Is a Process Sometimes students make inferences based on unsubstantiated assumptions or shoddy reasoning. Thoughtful inference strategies teach students the ongoing process of using evidence to test and refine their hypotheses and ideas.	**Phase Three: *F*ormulate and Refine Hypotheses** Teach students how to • Establish a hypothesis. • Collect evidence. • Refine their hypotheses in light of new findings.
Principle Four: You've Got Some Explaining to Do Inferential thinking shouldn't be hidden in students' minds. Instead, it needs to be articulated, refined, and applied. Thoughtful inference strategies require students to turn their thinking into clear explanations.	**Phase Four: *E*xplain Your Thinking** • Encourage discussion throughout the lesson that challenges students to explain their ideas and cite evidence. • Provide a synthesis task that helps students demonstrate what they've learned and explain the thinking they used.
Principle Five: Look Back to Move Forward Deep learning requires metacognition, or thinking about thinking (Costa & Kallick, 2008, 2009). If we expect students to become thoughtful inference makers, then we need to provide them with opportunities to reflect on their learning and thinking processes.	**Phase Five: *R*eflect on the Process** Allow students to step back and review the inference strategy they used to see how the process helped them and how they might use it again.

The Strategy in Action

Now let's experience a complete inference lesson designed by a teacher. Jason Mantzoukas designed this Inductive Learning lesson on what life was like in Colonial New England for the 9th graders in his U.S. history class. Inductive Learning helps students see the connections among pieces of information and construct, on their own, the broader perspective into which these pieces fit. Jason uses Inductive Learning to help students form and test hypotheses about life in Colonial New England and to address key reading and writing standards from the Common Core State Standards, including the following:

- [R.CCR.1] Read closely to determine what the text says explicitly and to make logical inferences from it; cite specific textual evidence when writing or speaking to support conclusions drawn from the text.
- [W.CCR.1] Write arguments to support claims in an analysis of substantive topics or texts, using valid reasoning and relevant and sufficient evidence.

A Model Lesson: Life in Colonial New England

Note to participants: As you review this lesson, keep in mind the principles of the inference strategy, the role of the students, the role of the teacher, and the goals of inference strategies. We also encourage you to *be* the student by completing the student activities throughout the lesson. You'll notice that we have included "You Try It" activities throughout. This is part of the process we call "Do, Look, Learn," which puts the power of metacognition, or thinking about thinking, to work. Too often, we go through the motions of learning a new strategy or technique without reflecting on our own thought process. So, as you "do" the lesson, "look" in on your own thought process and see what you can "learn" from your own experiences.

Phase One: *I*dentify What You Need to Figure Out

Jason begins the lesson by asking students, "Have you ever had a hunch? Did your hunch turn out to be right?" After a brief discussion, Jason continues: "Historians make hunches all the time. They call their hunches *hypotheses*. Along the way, they gather evidence that helps them support their hypotheses, refine them, or discard them and form new hypotheses altogether. Today we're going to use a strategy called Inductive Learning to help us develop hypotheses about Colonial New England." Jason explains that students will be examining words closely, dividing the words into labeled groups, and using those groups to develop hypotheses about Colonial New England. To set the scene, Jason says, "Imagine that you stepped into a time machine and wound up in Colonial New England. What do you suppose ordinary people might be talking about? What are some words or phrases you might expect to hear?"

You Try It: Generating Words

Work with your learning club to generate some words and phrases that you might hear in Colonial New England.

Phase Two: *Note* Information Sources and Look for Patterns

Jason surveys his students' ideas and then presents them with a word list that he has put together (see Figure 1.8).

Figure 1.8 Colonial New England Word List

spinning wheels	cornmeal	ashcakes	taxes
hoecakes	death penalty	breads	Sabbath
imported	smoked	salted	dried
breeches	cellars	linen	gentry
pillory	woven	faith	stocks
merchants	ducking stool	overcoats	church
planters	leather	leggings	lawyers
baptisms	wool	worship	farmers
fireplace	petticoats	prayer	shift
craftsmen	cattle	town meetings	homemade
hogs	laborers	hunted	Bible
slaves	deer	sin	servants
barrels	trap	oil lamps	squirrels
candles	governor	tinderboxes	clams
piety	lobsters	iron pots	

Jason reviews any words on the list that students are not familiar with and then explains that these words are all clues about what life was like in Colonial New England. Jason notes about the lesson, "After I showed students the words, I told them that we needed to find a way to organize the words if we were going to develop some good, reliable hypotheses. So I showed them how to use circles and labels to group terms that went together."

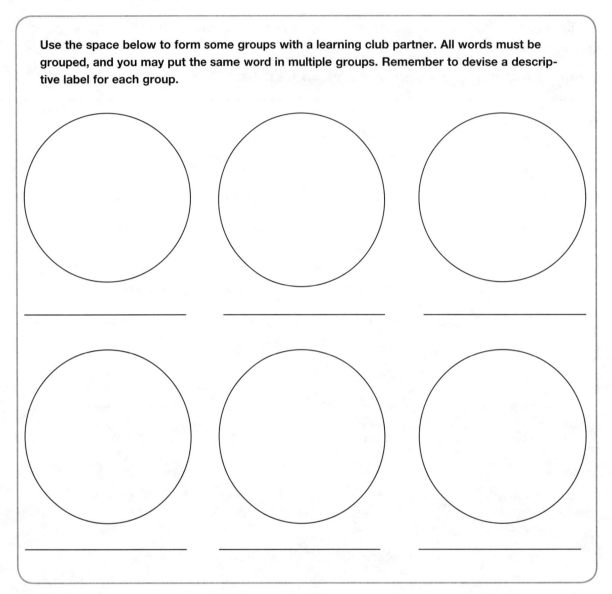

Use the space below to form some groups with a learning club partner. All words must be grouped, and you may put the same word in multiple groups. Remember to devise a descriptive label for each group.

Phase Three: *Formulate and Refine Hypotheses*

According to Jason, "The next part was a little harder. After students discussed their groups, I reminded them that historians call their hunches 'hypotheses.' I told them that a hypothesis was a sentence that might be true. Then, after some quick modeling, we worked together to use one or more groups to create a hypothesis. Students then worked in pairs to develop and record three hypotheses in a three-column organizer."

You Try It: Generating Hypotheses

Working with your learning club partner, use your word groups to generate three hypotheses in the first column of the organizer below.

Hypothesis	Support	Refute

Next, Jason gives students a reading to help them test out their ideas (see Figure 1.9, p. 26). Students collect evidence from the reading that either confirms or challenges their hypotheses and record the evidence in the "Support" or the "Refute" column of their organizers.

You Try It: Collecting Evidence

Read the passage in Figure 1.9. Work with your learning club to collect evidence that supports or refutes each hypothesis you listed in your organizer. Record your evidence in the appropriate column of the organizer.

Figure 1.9 What Was Life Like in Colonial New England?

When people first began colonizing New England, they retained the customs of the Old World and tried to replicate it in their everyday lives. Colonists thought, spoke, dressed, and generally acted as though they were an extension of England. Their society was structured like European society, with several classes of people. At the top of the social structure were the "gentry," made up of wealthy merchants, planters, lawyers, and doctors. Below the gentry were those who owned property but were not wealthy, including farmers, shopkeepers, and craftsmen. The bottom level consisted of poor, unskilled laborers who were generally slaves or contracted servants. The biggest difference between the social structure in the colonies and the structure in England was mobility. In the colonies, unless you were a slave, it was possible to rise to a higher class.

England controlled the government of the colonies. Each colony had a governor appointed by the king. Local governments were in charge of law enforcement, collecting taxes, and repairing roads. The death penalty was customary for crimes of armed robbery, counterfeiting, murder, and treason. Drunkenness, slander, swearing, theft, and breaking the Sabbath were considered minor offenses. The punishment for these crimes might be public whipping or public humiliation, such as being placed in the pillory, the stocks, or the ducking stool.

Domestic life in the New England colonies also developed from old European ways. The households were large and generally included resident in-laws. All members of the family were the responsibility of the father, who made all important decisions. The first houses were modeled after those in Europe, but later houses were built to adapt to local weather conditions and available materials. The life of the house centered on the fireplace, which provided the heat and light needed for everyday living. Much of the detail and design of a home, as well as lifestyle in general, depended on individual wealth. The wealthy imported fine furniture from Europe, but most colonists supplemented the few things they were able to bring from Europe with homemade items. The homemade furniture was plain and sturdy and made from available wood like pine and oak. Blocks of wood, barrels, or benches served as chairs. Colonists used oil lamps and candles for additional lighting. Tinderboxes, bed warmers, iron pots, and spinning wheels were generally considered necessities.

Clothing varied according to wealth and occupation. The wealthy imported clothes or had them tailored to resemble current European styles. On farms, workingmen wore breeches and long shirts made from linen woven by the women of the household. Male servants who worked in the field likely wore only breeches. In cold weather, the men wore loose-fitting overcoats, leather leggings, mittens, and wool caps. Women wore dresses, petticoats, and a single undergarment called a shift.

Most New Englanders had small farms located near villages or small towns. They raised cattle, hogs, sheep, and chickens, and they grew fruits and vegetables. From the local woods, they hunted deer and other game and trapped smaller animals like squirrels. They also fished the rivers and oceans and even collected clams and lobsters. Corn became a basic food in most households. Cornmeal was made into ashcakes, hoecakes, and breads. Storing food for the winter was a problem because colonists had no means to can or refrigerate food. Meats were smoked, salted, and dried. Colonists dug cellars to keep roots, fruits, and vegetables, but the usual winter diet consisted of bread and meat.

Religion and faith strongly influenced social and political life in the New England colonies. Many people came to the colonies seeking religious freedom. Church officials did the work that local governments take care of today, including education, care of the poor, and recordkeeping of marriages, baptisms, and deaths. The churches were not just sites of worship but also places for community gatherings and town meetings. The rules of the church generally became the laws of the colony.

Figure 1.9 What Was Life Like in Colonial New England? (*continued*)

> These rules were based on a strict interpretation of the Bible and were generally designed to keep people from sinning. Many everyday tasks like cooking, shaving, and other domestic activities were forbidden on Sunday. A life of piety and prayer was considered ideal.
>
> In time, the New England colonies developed their own way of life as they adapted to conditions in the New World. The men and women who had at one time viewed their colony as an extension of England began to consider themselves Americans.

Phase Four: *E*xplain Your Thinking

After students collect their evidence, Jason leads a discussion on how they did it and what they found, making sure to ask probing questions and positively reinforce students' use of specific evidence from the text.

You Try It: Discussing the Process

> **With your entire learning club, take a few minutes to talk about the process of gathering evidence to support hypotheses. Were your hypotheses correct? Did you need to refine them? What evidence did you find for each of your hypotheses?**

Says Jason, "One thing I try to do with my synthesis tasks is align them with the Common Core State Standards and the kinds of writing tasks that students face on state tests. For this lesson, I decided to bring the lesson home by having students write an argument, or thesis essay. I asked students to take a position by arguing either for or against the statement 'Life in Colonial New England was very different from life in England.' Then I reviewed the RESPONSE process [see Figure 1.10], which I use to help students internalize the steps in writing an effective thesis essay."

Figure 1.10 The RESPONSE Process

> **R**ead the question or writing prompt slowly and carefully.
>
> **E**stablish the purpose for writing. (Explain a concept? Describe a procedure? Argue a point?)
>
> **S**tart by introducing your topic or thesis. Be as clear and concise as possible.
>
> **P**rovide evidence, reasons, or examples to support your opening statement. (Address conflicting evidence or arguments if appropriate.)
>
> **O**rganize your supporting information (group related ideas, link ideas using transitions, etc.).
>
> **N**ail your ending. Write a conclusion that follows from, sums up, or reiterates your main point(s).
>
> **S**kim your draft for errors (spelling, grammar, logic), unclear terms/ideas, and "rough" writing.
>
> **E**dit and polish your original response.
>
> *Source:* Adapted from *Tools for Thoughtful Assessment,* by A. L. Boutz, H. F. Silver, J. W. Jackson, and M. J. Perini, 2012, Ho-Ho-Kus, NJ: Thoughtful Education Press. © 2012 Silver Strong & Associates/Thoughtful Education Press. Used with permission.

Jason notes about one student's work, "Take a close look at Geoffrey's essay [see Figure 1.11]. You can see he's got the RESPONSE process down: his thesis is clear, he's got three big ideas and evidence to support each one, and his conclusion is strong. The one thing we still need to work on as a class is responding to counterarguments. Once Geoffrey gets in the habit of responding to counterarguments, he'll be ready to handle an argument-based item on our state test."

Figure 1.11 Geoffrey's Essay

Not very much was "new" about Colonial New England. Despite the new territory and harsh conditions, New England copied the culture and society of England.

The colonies belonged to England and were controlled by the king. Governors were hired by the king for each colony and legislators were either elected or appointed. Through these appointed governments, England was able to tax and profit off the land.

The society of the early New England colonies was very similar to the society of England. The wealthiest members of society were the merchants, lawyers, and doctors. Beneath them were farmers and other small land owners, and the poorest of society were peasants and slaves. Since the rich were so rich and the poor were so poor, luxuries were only for the wealthy. Nearly all luxuries were imported from England. Popular fashions were English fashions, popular furniture was English furniture.

While many colonists left Europe in search of religious freedom, Christianity remained very influential in Colonial New England. The church was in charge of education, kept official records of marriages, baptisms, and deaths, and took care of the poor. The church was also very influential in politics. Many laws were created by the church. Skipping the Sabbath was a crime punishable by whipping or public humiliation, as were minor things like swearing or slander.

Though in time things would change, life in the English colonies was, not surprisingly, English. From its government to its churches, its laws to its fashion trends, this new world was very much like the old one.

Phase Five: *Reflect* on the Process

After Jason's class completes the lesson, he brings the whole thing to a close by hanging up his new inference poster (included with this PLC Guide) and asking students to think of other situations in which they could apply the INFER process.

ThoughtWork

Before the Next Section

Take a moment to reflect on what you have learned so far by answering the questions below.

Activity: Reflecting on Section 1

1. How did Jason's lesson support his students' abilities to think inferentially?

2. Looking over the lesson, how might you adapt or refine it to make it stronger?

3. Inductive Learning is one of four strategies that support and develop students' skills in inference. How might you use Inductive Learning in your own classroom?

ThoughtWork

In the next section, you will be planning your own inference lesson. To prepare, you should do the following things before you move on:

- Keep an eye out for situations in which students are thinking inferentially or might be asked to think inferentially.
  - Ask yourself, "How comfortable are my students in these situations?"
  - Jot down some examples of these situations to share with your learning club.
  - Preview the planning process in the next section (pp. 49–66). Compile all the materials you'll need to plan an inference lesson (e.g., content, standards to address) and bring them to the next learning club meeting.

Planning a Lesson

The goal in this section is to work with a partner to develop an inference lesson for your students.

In this section you will

■ Examine and learn from sample lessons and planning forms designed by other teachers.

■ Plan a complete inference lesson for your classroom.

■ Learn classroom tips to ensure highly effective implementation of the inference lesson in your classroom.

Samples of Inference Lessons

The following activity is designed to increase each learning club member's sense of responsibility for learning by making each an "expert" in one part of the content. The experts then meet to share their acquired knowledge.

On the following pages, you will find a matrix organizer (Figure 2.1) followed by four different inference lessons: an Inductive Learning lesson on a folktale titled "Spiders and Diamonds," designed by an elementary school teacher; a Mystery lesson on the extinction of the dinosaurs, designed by a high school science teacher; a Main Idea lesson designed for emerging primary-level readers; and an Investigation lesson designed by a 6th grade mathematics teacher. Here's how you and your learning club will use these resources to complete this activity:

1. Form a team with two other members of your learning club.
2. Read "Sample Lesson 1: Elementary Language Arts." Together, review the completed column for this lesson in Figure 2.1. You and your partners will be completing the remaining three columns.
3. Assign each of the remaining three lessons to a different member of the team.
4. Read your assigned lesson carefully. As you read it, underline key ideas, phrases, and interesting points. Use the Window Notes organizer below to collect ideas and make a set of notes that will help you teach what you have read back to your partners.
5. Rejoin your partners. Each of you will teach the content of your assigned sample lesson to the other partners. As team members explain their lessons, the group should work together to complete each column of the matrix organizer (Figure 2.1).

Activity: Window Notes for Your Sample Lesson

Compose a concise summary (three or fewer sentences) of how the inference strategy used in your lesson works.	**How might you use this strategy in your classroom?**
How does your lesson build students' inference skills?	**Create a headline for your lesson.**

Figure 2.1 Activity: Matrix Organizer for Sample Inference Lessons

	Lesson 1: Inductive Learning	Lesson 2: Mystery	Lesson 3: Main Idea	Lesson 4: Investigation
Summary	Students group words from a folk-tale and label their groups. They make three predictions and test them against the actual reading. The class discusses both the story and the process.			
How It Builds Inference Skills	Students • Make connections between words. • Form and test predictions. • Collect evidence. • Draw conclusions and discuss them.			
Headline	"Predictions lead to deeper reading."			
Use in Your Classroom	I might try this out with an important historical document. The strategy would work well with the Gettysburg Address or "Letter from Birmingham Jail."			

Inductive Learning

Phase One: *Identify What You Need to Figure Out*

Art Espinoza knows that when students make predictions about a text, their reading becomes an active search for evidence. Today, as part of his unit on folktales, Art wants students to form predictions about a short folktale called "Spiders and Diamonds." He has decided to use the Inductive Learning strategy. After a brief discussion in which students share their ideas on how good readers make and test predictions, Art introduces the Inductive Learning strategy and tells students that they will be examining words from a folktale. He tells students the title of the story before they read it so that they can make predictions about what will happen.

Phase Two: *Note Information Sources and Look for Patterns*

Art presents a list of key words and phrases to students (see Figure 2.2). "These words and phrases," he tells students, "are clues about the folktale we'll be reading."

Figure 2.2 Key Words and Phrases

mean	stupid	diamonds	window	share	friendly
kind	spiders	digging	listening	possessions	repay
helping	forest	talking	old woman	shattered	nosy
beggar	chimney	dinner	old man	rusty shovel	eat
selfish man	search	apple tree	food	treasure	glass jar

Art models the grouping-and-labeling process by creating a few sample groups, explaining to students how he decides which words go together, and developing clear and simple labels for his groups. Figure 2.3 shows two of Art's sample groups.

Figure 2.3 Two Sample Groups and Labels

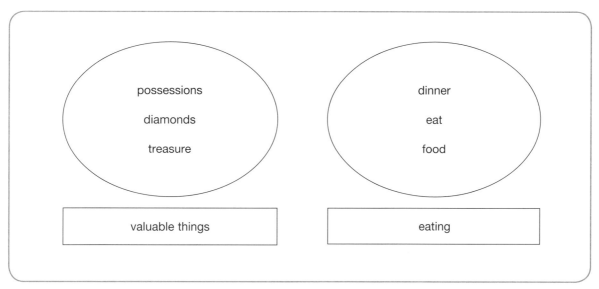

Next, Art divides students into teams of three to develop their own sets of groups and labels from the list of key words. He encourages students to be flexible in their thinking and to look for ways to merge groups or link them together. As students work, Art walks around the room, observing teams at work and coaching those who are struggling. After the teams have created their initial labeled groups, Art calls the teams together, and the class as a whole works to create a comprehensive set of groups and labels like those shown in Figure 2.4 (p. 36).

Figure 2.4 Groups and Labels

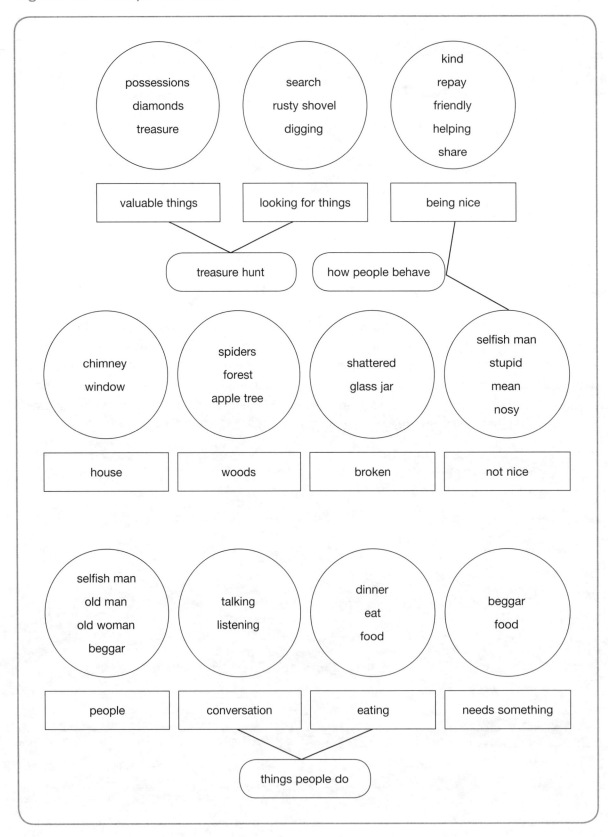

Phase Three: *Formulate and Refine Hypotheses (Predictions)*

With the completed groups and labels under their belts, students are ready to make predictions. Art asks students to look over their labeled groups and use them to make predictions about all aspects of the story, including the characters, the setting, the action, the problem, and the resolution of the problem. As students share their predictions, Art records them on the board:

1. The story takes place in the woods and in a house.
2. The characters are a selfish man, an old man, an old woman, and a beggar.
3. The beggar needs food to eat.
4. A selfish man was mean to the beggar.
5. The people were digging in the woods for treasure.
6. The selfish man is stupid and mean to the beggar, the old man, and the old woman.

Next, Art distributes copies of "Spiders and Diamonds," along with a three-column prediction organizer (see Figure 2.5).

Figure 2.5 Prediction Organizer

Evidence That Supports	Predictions	Evidence That Refutes

Students record their three favorite predictions in the middle column and then read the folktale on their own. As they read, they collect evidence that either supports or refutes each prediction and record it in the appropriate column of the organizer.

Spiders and Diamonds

A kind old man and woman lived in a house by the forest. They had few possessions, but they were happy with what they had. A mean, selfish man lived nearby. He had many possessions, but he always wanted more. One day, a beggar came to the mean man's house and asked for food. The mean man asked why he should share his food. He laughed and threw the beggar out of his house. The beggar then went to the house of the kind people. They invited him to eat dinner with them. They told him that they were poor and did not have much food, but that he was welcome to the little that they did have.

After dinner, the beggar told the kind old man and woman that he wanted to repay them for being so friendly. He told them that they could find treasure by digging under the old apple tree in the forest. The woman said it was too late to go digging for treasure. Everyone agreed, and they all decided to go to sleep and search for the treasure in the morning.

The selfish man was also a nosy man. He had been standing outside the window of the kind old couple's house, listening to them talking. As soon as he heard about the treasure, he ran home to get his rusty shovel and then went straight into the forest to the old apple tree. He dug all around the tree. He dug for hours, until he was so tired he could barely stand up. Finally, just as he was about to give up, he found a jar. But when he picked it up, all he saw inside were thousands of tiny spiders.

The selfish man was very angry. He was tired, and because he was so mean, he wanted to get back at the old couple. He thought the old couple was stupid for helping the beggar when all he could do to repay them was tell them where to find a jar of spiders. So, when he reached the house of the kind old couple, he threw the jar of spiders down the chimney. When the jar hit the floor of their tiny living room, it shattered. But the spiders inside the glass jar were no longer spiders. All those thousands of spiders had turned into diamonds!

Phase Four: *E*xplain Your Thinking

After students have read the story, Art leads a class discussion on which predictions were most accurate and why. As a culminating task, Art divides students into teams and provides each team with a different short folktale. Teams select 20 words or phrases from their folktales that they believe will help a reader make predictions about the characters, setting, problem, action, and resolution. Teams then exchange their word lists and use them to make predictions about one another's folktales before testing the predictions against the text.

Phase Five: *R*eflect on the Process

Finally, Art uses the INFER poster (included with this guide) to reinforce the inference process with students. Together, Art and his students connect what happened during the lesson to each step in the INFER process. Art also encourages students to identify which steps gave them the most trouble and to explore ideas for overcoming these problems next time.

Mystery

Phase One: *I*dentify What You Need to Figure Out

Marcy Jereau wants her students to solve problems the way real scientists do, by thinking analytically and inferentially. As part of her unit on evolution and adaptation, she has decided to challenge students to figure out the reasons behind the extinction of the dinosaurs and why mammals survived the same changes that killed off the dinosaurs. Marcy sets the scene by asking students to close their eyes and imagine that they've been transported 10 million years into the future. She paints images of exotic creatures roaming the planet. Then she reveals to students that humans no longer exist.

After students share their ideas on how and why humans disappeared from Earth, Marcy explains that the dinosaurs dominated the planet for more than 160 million years. She then presents the mystery that will guide the lesson: Why did the dinosaurs, the dominant life form on Earth, disappear completely? And why did other animals, like mammals, survive?

By presenting the content this way, Marcy aims for students to discover—rather than be told—three big ideas:

- **Big Idea #1:** Dinosaurs dominated life on Earth for more than 160 million years. *Homo sapiens* have been around for only 250,000 years. Dinosaurs thrived on all of the continents and in every kind of climate. But by the end of the Cretaceous period (about 70 million years ago), they were completely extinct.
- **Big Idea #2:** A giant asteroid hit the Earth, causing a vast dust cloud to block the sun and thereby create a dramatic climate change.
- **Big Idea #3:** Due to the lack of sun, trees and plants dwindled. Animals were dying off, and the food chain was breaking down. With limited food available, smaller, quicker mammals had an advantage that allowed them to survive.

Phase Two: *N*ote Information Sources and Look for Patterns

To help students discover the big ideas behind dinosaur extinction, Marcy presents her class with a "deck" of 30 clues. These clues are bits of information taken from an article and include facts, a map, a time line, and several images. Marcy's goal is to have students begin to see the bigger picture by grouping related clues together. For example, here are two groups of related clues:

Group 1: Dinosaur Eggs

- Some mammals ate eggs.
- Many species of dinosaurs were especially protective of their eggs.
- Chickens under stress often lay eggs with thinner shells.
- Dinosaur eggs became thinner toward the end of the Cretaceous period.

Group 2: Cycads

- A principal food for plant-eating dinosaurs was large tropical plants known as *cycads*.
- Cycads declined rapidly during the late Cretaceous period.
- Cycads need high temperatures day and night to survive.

Phase Three: *Formulate and Refine Hypotheses*

Marcy divides the class into teams of three students who will work together to create clue groups, develop a set of main ideas, and generate a hypothesis about why the dinosaurs became extinct while many mammals survived. As students work, Marcy moves around the room, listening in on groups to assess the quality of their thinking, helping groups that are struggling, and challenging students to test their hypotheses against the clues. She has students record their main ideas and hypotheses using an organizer like the one in Figure 2.6. Students are asked to evaluate their hypotheses against the article.

Figure 2.6 Main Idea/Hypothesis Organizer

3 Main Ideas

Main Idea 1:

Clues that support this idea:

Main Idea 2:

Clues that support this idea:

Main Idea 3:

Clues that support this idea:

Hypothesis: _____

_____

_____

Phase Four: *Explain Your Thinking*

When Marcy is satisfied that students have a solid understanding of the main ideas in the article, she asks students to draft a brief essay explaining why mammals survived the changes that destroyed the dinosaurs. Students refine their essays together in their groups, and then each group presents its best final essay to the class.

Phase Five: *Reflect on the Process*

Marcy helps students examine their learning experience through a discussion driven by these questions:

- Before this lesson, did you understand what happened to the dinosaurs?
- Do you feel as though you understand the theory set forth in the article? What evidence can you cite to back up your conclusions?

After the discussion, Marcy previews the next lesson in the unit, telling students that they will conduct a lab experiment in which they will test bacteria's resistance to antibiotics. "So," Marcy says, "who has any ideas about how what we just learned about dinosaurs and mammals might relate to bacteria's resistance to antibiotics?"

Main Idea

Phase One: *I*dentify What You Need to Figure Out

Russell Freeley knows how important it is for young readers to be able to identify main ideas. That's why he uses the Main Idea strategy regularly in his classroom. Today, he is introducing the strategy to 1st graders as they read about some of the games children played in Ancient Egypt.

"Have you ever read something and been a little confused about what you're reading?" Russell asks students. "It happens to me sometimes, and when it does, I like to use a strategy called Main Idea to help me figure out what the reading is all about. Who can tell me what a main idea is?" After a few minutes of discussion, Russell poses the following question to students: "What if you were an idea and wanted to become a main idea? What are some things you might do to get noticed?"

Phase Two: *N*ote Information Sources and Look for Patterns

After collecting students' thoughts about main ideas, Russell passes out copies of the reading. "As we read, we'll be looking for clues to help us figure out what the main idea of the reading is." Russell pulls up a Main Idea Organizer (see Figure 2.7, p. 44) on the interactive whiteboard and tells students, "The first thing we do when we use the Main Idea strategy is to hunt for words and phrases that seem like they're important." Russell reads the text aloud while students follow along, stopping to write important words and phrases on the "Key Words/Phrases" part of the organizer. Then he reads the text aloud a second time. This time, he asks students to add words and phrases that seem important to them. As students offer up words and phrases, Russell adds them to the organizer.

Next, Russell says, "Now that we've collected some important words and phrases, we need to ask ourselves, 'What is the topic of this reading?' In other words, what is this reading all about?"

"Games," one student offers.

"Yes, games," says Russell. "Are they particular kinds of games or just any old games?"

"They're all Ancient Egyptian games," says another student.

Russell writes "Ancient Egyptian games" in the "Topic" oval of the organizer.

Phase Three: *Formulate and Refine Hypotheses (Main Idea)*

Now Russell asks his class, "What is the main idea of this reading? What is it telling us about the topic of Ancient Egyptian games?" After a number of students offer up their ideas, the class comes to an agreement that the main idea of the reading is "Ancient Egyptian children played games that are like some games children play today." Russell writes the main idea in the organizer.

"So, are we done?" asks Russell. "Not quite yet. Because now we have to be good thinkers by testing our main idea to see whether it stands up to the details in the reading. What details in the reading seem to support the main idea that Ancient Egyptian games are similar to some of your games?"

"They had games with pieces and dice."

"Yeah, like some of our board games."

"They had sports like swimming and running."

"They had all kinds of toys."

As students offer up details that support the main idea, Russell records them in the "Supporting Details" portion of the Main Idea organizer.

Figure 2.7 Main Idea Organizer

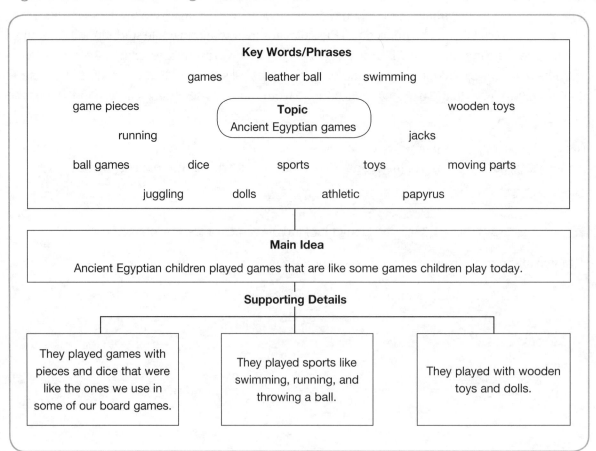

Phase Four: *Explain Your Thinking*

To synthesize the lesson, Russell asks students to complete a single-paragraph sequence essay explaining to a student who has never heard of the Main Idea strategy how to find a main idea. Students' essays follow a simple format:

Today we used a strategy called_____ to find a main idea. The main idea

we found was: _____

_____

_____

Here's how you can find a main idea: First, you_____

_____

_____

Next, you_____

_____

_____

Then, you_____

_____

_____

Finally, you _____

_____

_____

Phase Five: *Reflect on the Process*

To help students use the Main Idea strategy independently, Russell has created a poster that presents four questions:

1. What words or phrases seem important?
2. What or who is the focus of the reading?
3. What is the reading telling me about this topic?
4. What details in the reading support my main idea?

Students use the poster throughout the year as they hunt for main ideas.

Investigation

Phase One: *I*dentify What You Need to Figure Out

Sandra Nguyen has created a mathematics investigation (adapted from Hynes, 2004) on measurement for her 6th grade mathematics class. The investigation is designed to develop her students' measurement and data-analysis skills, as well as their ability to design an experiment. To conduct the investigation, students will be testing the strength of paper tubes.

Sandra begins the investigation by asking her students to generate a "Fist List" of five things that come to mind when they think of the concept *strength*. After she collects some ideas and probes students' responses, the class arrives at a definition, agreeing that strength is a measure of the ability to lift or hold something.

Sandra then holds up a piece of paper and poses the following three questions to the class:

1. How strong is this paper?
2. How would you go about measuring the strength of the paper?
3. What could you do to increase the paper's strength?

After allowing students some time to consider the three questions, she breaks them up into groups and explains that their task is to design an experiment that will test the weight-bearing capacity of a paper tube when it is horizontal and bridging an eight-inch space.

Phase Two: *N*ote Information Sources and Look for Patterns

Before the students begin to design their experiments, Sandra instructs them to brainstorm what variables could be manipulated that might affect the strength of the paper tube. Students' proposed variables include length of the tube, thickness of the paper, and circumference of the tube.

Next, Sandra provides each group with paper, scissors, tape, glue, paper clips, weights, string, and containers (paper cups). Each group brainstorms how it can use the materials to test the strength of paper tubes of various lengths and circumferences. One group proposes the design depicted in Figure 2.8. Students from this group place the paper tube between two desks and hang the container from the tube to see how much weight the tube can hold.

Figure 2.8 Design of Paper Tube Experiment

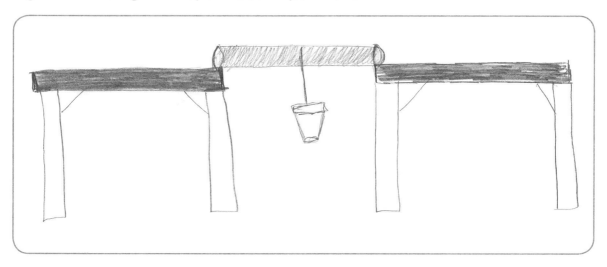

Sandra also challenges each group to develop a form for collecting data from the experiments. One group creates the chart shown in Figure 2.9. Using this group's chart as a model, Sandra leads a discussion on how students will record crucial information.

Figure 2.9 Data Chart for Tube Experiment

	Circumference of Tube	Length of Tube	Weight the Tube Supports
Trial 1			
Trial 2			
Trial 3			
Trial 4			
Trial 5			
Trial 6			

Phase Three: *F*ormulate and Refine Hypotheses

Once the groups' experimental designs and data collection forms have been approved, Sandra asks them to generate some tentative hypotheses about the effects that the tube's length and circumference would have on its weight-bearing capacity. The groups then begin experimenting while Sandra observes.

Phase Four: *E*xplain Your Thinking

After the student groups collect their data, they discuss what makes a tube strong. Each group must make some generalizations about the paper tube's circumference and length, and how these variables affect the maximum weight the tube can support.

After the discussion, Sandra tells her students that they will be participating in a contest to create the paper tube that holds the most weight. Students must use the results of their experiments to design a tube that applies the principles they have learned. Sandra uses a balance with standardized weights to assess the results of each group's work.

Phase Five: *R*eflect on the Process

Sandra asks students to create a journal entry reflecting on the importance of accuracy and precision in measurement when designing experiments.

Planning an Inference Lesson

Now it's time to plan your own inference lesson. To help you plan your lesson, we have included the planning forms completed by the four teachers whose lessons you have just examined. Because there is one set of completed planning forms for each of the four inference strategies (Inductive Learning, Mystery, Main Idea, and Investigation), you can refer to the planning forms you need once you decide which strategy you will be using.

Teacher Talk: A Word About Purpose

When you look at the teachers' planning forms for the sample lessons, you'll notice that each used a special framework for defining the purpose of his or her lesson that looks like this:

Knowledge	Habits of Mind[*]
What key information and facts do students need to know?	What habits of mind do you want to foster?
Understanding	**Skills**
What big ideas, generalizations, or principles do students need to understand?	What skills do students need to develop?

We call this framework a *learning window* (Silver & Perini, 2010), and we have found that using it to "unpack" standards and clarify purpose leads to richer, more integrated, and better-designed lessons.

[*]For a complete list of the 16 habits of mind, see Appendix B (p. 109).

Figure 2.10 Sample Planning Form: Inductive Learning Lesson (Elementary Language Arts)

Step 1: Identify the Purpose of the Lesson and the Inference Strategy You Will Be Using

What standards will you be addressing?

For this lesson on reading a folktale, I'll be addressing these Common Core State Standards:

[RL.3.1]: Ask and answer questions to demonstrate understanding of a text, referring explicitly to the text as the basis for the answers.

[RL.3.2]: Recount stories, including fables, folktales, and myths from diverse cultures; determine the central message, lesson, or moral and explain how it is conveyed through key details in the text.

[RL.3.4]: Determine the meaning of words and phrases as they are used in a text, distinguishing literal from nonliteral language.

Clarify your purpose by converting your standards into clear learning targets.

Knowledge	Habits of Mind
Students will know	*Students will develop the habits of*
• The components of a folktale, including characters, setting, actions, problem, and resolution.	• Thinking flexibly. • Applying past knowledge to new situations.
Understanding	**Skills**
Students will understand	*Students will be able to*
• That good readers make predictions before reading and test them during reading.	• Group words and phrases. • Make and test predictions.

Which inference strategy will best address your standards and targets? Why?

I'll definitely be using Inductive Learning. It is all about helping students make and test predictions.

Figure 2.10 (*continued*)

Step 2: Identify Information Sources and What You Expect Students to Discover

What information sources will students use?

The first source of information will be the terms selected from the folktale. I want words that will really help students create some strong images in their minds. The terms also need to suggest meaningful groups. The terms I'll give them include

- Characters (e.g., selfish man, old man, beggar, old woman).
- Setting terms (e.g., apple tree, chimney, window, dinner).
- Action terms (e.g., search, digging, share, talking, helping, shattered, eat, repay).
- Important objects (e.g., glass jar, spiders, rusty shovel, possessions, treasure, food).
- Descriptive adjectives (e.g., stupid, mean, nosy, selfish, friendly, kind).

Later in the lesson, students will read the actual folktale.

What big ideas and key details do you want students to discover?

I want students to form some good predictions after analyzing and grouping the terms. Their predictions don't need to be correct, just well formulated on the basis of the terms. Then students will check their predictions against the text, collecting evidence that supports or refutes their predictions.

What kind of organizer will students use to make sense of the information?

Two organizers:

1. A group-and-label organizer for students to group terms and assign labels.	2. A prediction organizer for students to record predictions and collect evidence.

Evidence For	Predictions	Evidence Against

Figure 2.10 (*continued*)

Step 3: Determine How Students Will Interact with the Information

How will you introduce and model the strategy for students?

I'll walk the class through the strategy, step by step. I'll model the group-and-label process by creating some simple groups for them to see. For example:

possessions

diamonds

treasure

| valuable things |

dinner

eat

food

| eating |

What will the process look like?

Will students work alone, in groups, as a class with you leading, or a combination?

I'll lead in the beginning, but they'll do a lot of the actual work in small groups.

What will your role be while students work?

I'll be leading the class through the steps. While students are reading and collecting evidence and while they're working on their final tasks, I'll circulate to observe and listen in. Good formative assessment opportunity!

Figure 2.10 (*continued*)

Step 4: Decide How Students Will Demonstrate What They Have Learned

How will you assess the quality of student thinking?

Hold a discussion on "most accurate prediction." Probe students' responses with questions like

- Why is this a good prediction?
- What evidence in the story supports it?
- How do descriptive words help us make predictions about characters, setting, etc.?
- How might you use this process on your own?
- How is reading a form of making predictions?

How will students apply what they've learned?

I'll break students into teams and give each team a short folktale. Each team will select 20 words or phrases from its folktale that it believes will help a reader make predictions about the characters, setting, problem, action, and resolution. Teams will then exchange their word lists and use them to make predictions about one another's folktales before testing their predictions against the stories.

Figure 2.10 (*continued*)

Step 5: Develop the Hook and the Reflection Activity

What kind of "hook" or interesting question/activity will you use before the lesson to engage students and activate their prior knowledge?

We'll open with a discussion on predictions:

- Have you ever made a prediction? Did it turn out to be right?
- What is a prediction? What makes some predictions better than others?
- How do good readers make predictions?
- How do good readers check their predictions?

Then I'll bridge the discussion to the lesson.

What kinds of reflection activities/questions will you use after the lesson to help students make generalizations and/or transfer their learning?

I'll use the INFER poster to help students internalize how the process works and how they worked on each step. I'll also have them identify steps that gave them trouble and share their ideas for getting better at using the INFER process.

Figure 2.11 Sample Planning Form: Mystery Lesson (High School Science)

Step 1: Identify the Purpose of the Lesson and the Inference Strategy You Will Be Using

What standards will you be addressing?

This lesson on the dinosaurs will help me address key state standards for life science related to evolution, adaptation, and survival (or extinction) of organisms and species due to environmental change. I'll also have students present their hypotheses and evidence and compose an essay to address Common Core State Standards on explanatory writing (WHST.9-10.2) and collaborative discussion (SL.9-10.1).

Clarify your purpose by converting your standards into clear learning targets.

Knowledge	Habits of Mind
Students will know	*Students will develop the habits of*
The facts and background information surrounding the dinosaurs' extinction, including • When it happened. • How long dinosaurs dominated Earth. • Key vocabulary: Cretaceous period, asteroid, iridium, alkaloids, cycads, plankton.	• Thinking flexibly. • Questioning and posing problems.
Understanding	**Skills**
Students will understand	*Students will be able to*
• That life depends on complex environmental factors and relationships. • How and why the dinosaurs disappeared after dominating life on Earth for 160 million years. • How mammals' adaptations gave them an advantage.	• Find and support main ideas. • Develop and support a hypothesis. • Explain what happened to the dinosaurs and why many mammals survived.

Which inference strategy will best address your standards and targets? Why?

Mystery—it's perfect for what I'm trying to do. It forces students to construct and discover the answers themselves, like real scientists do.

Figure 2.11 (*continued*)

Step 2: Identify Information Sources and What You Expect Students to Discover

What information sources will students use?

Students will use the following information sources:

- An article, converted into brief clues. Clues will be one or two sentences long. A few clues will contain visual information (e.g., a time line, a map).
- Later in the lesson, students will read the actual article to evaluate their thinking and inferences.

What big ideas and key details do you want students to discover?

- **Big Idea #1:** Dinosaurs dominated life on Earth for more than 160 million years. *Homo sapiens* have been around for only 250,000 years. Dinosaurs thrived on all of the continents and in every kind of climate. But by the end of the Cretaceous period (about 70 million years ago), they were completely extinct.
- **Big Idea #2:** A giant asteroid hit the Earth, causing a vast dust cloud to block the sun and thereby create a dramatic climate change.
- **Big Idea #3:** Due to the lack of sun, trees and plants dwindled. Animals were dying off, and the food chain was breaking down. With limited food available, smaller, quicker mammals had an advantage that allowed them to survive.

What kind of organizer will students use to make sense of the information?

Students will group clues using a Main Idea/Hypothesis Organizer:

3 Main Ideas

Main Idea 1:
Clues That Support This Idea:

Main Idea 2:
Clues That Support This Idea:

Main Idea 3:
Clues That Support This Idea:

Hypothesis: _____

_____

_____

Figure 2.11 (*continued*)

Step 3: Determine How Students Will Interact with the Information

How will you introduce and model the strategy for students?

Depending on students' comfort level, I may work with the class to create a model grouping before they do groupings on their own.

What will the process look like?

Will students work alone, in groups, as a class with you leading, or a combination?

Students will mostly work in teams.

What will your role be while students work?

I'll explain the process, provide assistance, and walk around the room to observe students while they work.

Step 4: Decide How Students Will Demonstrate What They Have Learned

How will you assess the quality of student thinking?

Each group will present its main ideas, hypothesis, and supporting evidence.

How will students apply what they've learned?

I'll ask them to write essays explaining what happened to the dinosaurs and why many mammals survived the changes that killed off the dinosaurs.

Figure 2.11 (*continued*)

Step 5: Develop the Hook and the Reflection Activity

What kind of "hook" or interesting question/activity will you use before the lesson to engage students and activate their prior knowledge?

The lesson is a mystery with the intrigue built right in: How did the dinosaurs disappear after dominating the planet for more than 160 million years? And why did mammals survive? I'll play up the intrigue of that. To start, I'll ask students to visualize a future with no humans. How did they disappear? We can have some fun with that. Also, to put the 160 million years in context, I'll ask them how long *Homo sapiens* has been a dominant life form on Earth (been around for 250,000 years, dominated for about 70,000 years).

What kinds of reflection activities/questions will you use after the lesson to help students make generalizations and/or transfer their learning?

At the end of the lesson, I'll ask students to reflect on their learning with questions like these:

- Before this lesson, did you understand what happened to the dinosaurs?
- Do you understand what happened to them now?

I'll also introduce the next lesson, which is a lab experiment on bacteria and their resistance to antibiotics. I'll ask students whether they can make the connection between what they just learned and the lesson to come (adaptation/evolution, how organisms survive).

Figure 2.12 Sample Planning Form: Main Idea Lesson (Primary Social Studies)

Step 1: Identify the Purpose of the Lesson and the Inference Strategy You Will Be Using

What standards will you be addressing?

The article focuses on Ancient Egyptian games, but this lesson is all about helping students identify main ideas. I want to focus heavily on the Common Core State Standard for main idea: *Identify the main topic and retell key details of a text.* (RI.1.2)

I'll also do some work at the end of the lesson on sequence writing, which will help me address standard W.1.3 from the Common Core.

Clarify your purpose by converting your standards into clear learning targets.

Knowledge	Habits of Mind
Students will know	*Students will develop the habit of*
• Key details from the reading (i.e., the kinds of games that children played in Ancient Egypt).	• Thinking and communicating with clarity and precision.
Understanding	**Skills**
Students will understand	*Students will be able to*
• The main idea of the reading: The games children played in Ancient Egypt were a lot like the games children play today. • The difference between a topic and a main idea. • That readers test the strength of their main ideas against details in the reading.	• Construct and test a main idea. • Write a simple sequence essay telling how to find a main idea.

Which inference strategy will best address your standards and targets? Why?

I'm using the Main Idea strategy because it builds the skills of constructing and testing main ideas, which is what I'm after.

Figure 2.12 (*continued*)

Step 2: Identify Information Sources and What You Expect Students to Discover

What information sources will students use?

We'll be reading a grade-appropriate web article on the games and toys of Ancient Egyptian children. The article doesn't state the main idea directly, so it's ideal for teaching students how to use the Main Idea strategy—and inferential thinking—to construct a main idea.

What big ideas and key details do you want students to discover?

That the games Ancient Egyptian children played are a lot like many games kids play today.

What kind of organizer will students use to make sense of the information?

A Main Idea Organizer with three boxes for details. (We can add more if needed, but three feels doable for young readers.)

Key Words

Topic

Main Idea

──── **Supporting Details** ────

Figure 2.12 (*continued*)

Step 3: Determine How Students Will Interact with the Information

How will you introduce and model the strategy for students?

I'll be walking them through the strategy, step by step.

What will the process look like?

Will students work alone, in groups, as a class with you leading, or a combination?

Mostly as a class with me leading. Next time I use the strategy, I'll let them work together in small groups.

What will your role be while students work?

Guiding students through the strategy. Reading aloud. Assessing their understanding of the article and the process. Helping students who are struggling.

Step 4: Decide How Students Will Demonstrate What They Have Learned

How will you assess the quality of student thinking?

I'll use surveying and light discussion throughout the lesson to see how students are doing. As students work on their essays, I'll observe and provide coaching as needed.

How will students apply what they've learned?

I'll give them a preformatted sequence essay organizer. They'll write down the steps for finding a main idea in essay form.

Figure 2.12 (*continued*)

Step 5: Develop the Hook and the Reflection Activity

What kind of "hook" or interesting question/activity will you use before the lesson to engage students and activate their prior knowledge?

I'll start by talking about how I sometimes get confused about what I read and how the strategy can help. Then we'll review and deepen our understanding of what a main idea is with this little hook: What if you were an idea and wanted to become a main idea? What are some things you might do to get noticed?

What kinds of reflection activities/questions will you use after the lesson to help students make generalizations and/or transfer their learning?

I'll pose the four steps of the strategy as questions, and we'll talk about how we can use these questions to help us find main ideas in the future:

- What words or phrases seem important?
- Who or what is the focus of the reading?
- What is the reading telling me about the topic?
- What details in the reading support my main idea?

Also, as we use the strategy more often, I'll start to teach students about the different kinds of cues they can look for in a text that tell them when a word or phrase might be particularly important (e.g., boldface or italic font, headings, high frequency).

Figure 2.13 Sample Planning Form: Investigation Lesson (Middle School Mathematics)

Step 1: Identify the Purpose of the Lesson and the Inference Strategy You Will Be Using

What standards will you be addressing?

This lesson is a mathematical investigation. It will help students build the following key Standards for Mathematical Practice from the Common Core State Standards:

1. Make sense of problems and persevere in solving them.
2. Reason abstractly and quantitatively.
4. Model with mathematics.
5. Use appropriate tools strategically.
6. Attend to precision.

Clarify your purpose by converting your standards into clear learning targets.

Knowledge	Habits of Mind
Students will know	*Students will develop the habits of*
Key terms, including • Circumference. • Length. • Strength. • Accuracy. • Precision. • Experiment.	• Thinking interdependently. • Striving for accuracy. • Gathering data through all senses.
Understanding	**Skills**
Students will understand	*Students will be able to*
• The relationship among circumference, length, and strength. • That we can use mathematical experimentation to make better products. • The importance of accuracy and precision in experimentation.	• Design an experiment. • Collect important information. • Make a paper tube that applies what they've learned.

Which inference strategy will best address your standards and targets? Why?

Investigation. Students will be designing and conducting an experiment and collecting data from their investigation.

Figure 2.13 (*continued*)

Step 2: Identify Information Sources and What You Expect Students to Discover

What information sources will students use?

The information will come from the experiment itself. Students will be presented with the problem and these materials: paper, scissors, tape, glue, paper clips, weights, string, and containers (paper cups). They will be challenged to use these materials to design their own experiment and to generate and collect data.

What big ideas and key details do you want students to discover?

I want them to discover the "ideal tube" for weight-bearing through manipulation of circumference and length.

What kind of organizer will students use to make sense of the information?

I'll challenge them to design their own organizer, checking each group's design to make sure that it will help the group capture the critical information (length, circumference, weight supported).

I can also present one group's organizer as a model for the other groups.

Figure 2.13 (*continued*)

Step 3: Determine How Students Will Interact with the Information

How will you introduce and model the strategy for students?

I'll present the problem, but I don't want to model the experiment for students. The challenge will be for them to work together to design an experiment that will get them the information they need to make generalizations.

What will the process look like?

Will students work alone, in groups, as a class with you leading, or a combination?

This will be a cooperative lesson, with students working in small groups.

What will your role be while students work?

Set the problem up, then get out of the way. Of course, I'll be doing lots of observing and listening. If any students' organizers or experimental designs are off base, I'll provide guidance.

Step 4: Decide How Students Will Demonstrate What They Have Learned

How will you assess the quality of student thinking?

We'll be discussing what makes a tube strong and students' experimental designs. I'll also ask students to make some generalizations from their experiments.

How will students apply what they've learned?

We'll have an in-class challenge to create the paper tube that holds the most weight. Each group will present one final tube. I'll test each tube to see which one holds the most weight.

Figure 2.13 (*continued*)

Step 5: Develop the Hook and the Reflection Activity

What kind of "hook" or interesting question/activity will you use before the lesson to engage students and activate their prior knowledge?

I'll have students explore and rethink what the word *strength* means with a Fist List. On each finger, students write a word or phrase they associate with strength. Then we'll discuss their ideas and see if we can agree on a definition of strength.

What kinds of reflection activities/questions will you use after the lesson to help students make generalizations and/or transfer their learning?

I'll have them do some journal writing. They'll explore the importance of accuracy and precision in measurement when conducting experiments.

Inference Planning Forms

Now you are ready to design an inference lesson for your own classroom. You will be using the content you brought when you started this section to create the lesson. As you work through the planning forms that follow on pages 67–71, refer to the teachers' completed planning forms (Figures 2.10–2.13) as models. All four strategies (Inductive Learning, Mystery, Main Idea, and Investigation) are represented in the completed forms, so you can see the nuances of how each strategy is planned. We also recommend that you review the Classroom Tips (pp. 72–81) for the strategy you select before you begin the planning process. The Classroom Tips contain a wealth of suggestions and ideas for making sure your lesson works in the classroom. Remember to keep your students in mind and pay attention to what they will be doing during the different phases of the lesson. Use the poster included with this guide to help students understand their roles in an inference lesson and to help them see how they can use the strategy independently. (*Note: Although the INFER poster works for all four strategies discussed in this guide, it may not be the ideal way to introduce the Main Idea strategy, especially to young learners. The text for an alternate poster designed for use with the Main Idea strategy can be found on page 77.*)

Inference Planning Forms

What standards will you be addressing?

Clarify your purpose by converting your standards into clear learning targets.

Knowledge	Habits of Mind
Students will know	*Students will develop the habits of*
Understanding	**Skills**
Students will understand	*Students will be able to*

Which inference strategy will best address your standards and targets? Why?

Step 2: Identify Information Sources and What You Expect Students to Discover

What information sources will students use?

What big ideas and key details do you want students to discover?

What kind of organizer will students use to make sense of the information?

Step 3: Determine How Students Will Interact with the Information

How will you introduce and model the strategy for students?

What will the process look like?

Will students work alone, in groups, as a class with you leading, or a combination?

What will your role be while students work?

Step 4: Decide How Students Will Demonstrate What They Have Learned

How will you assess the quality of student thinking?

How will students apply what they've learned?

Step 5: Develop the Hook and the Reflection Activity

What kind of "hook" or interesting question/activity will you use before the lesson to engage students and activate their prior knowledge?

What kinds of reflection activities/questions will you use after the lesson to help students make generalizations and/or transfer their learning?

Classroom Tips

In this section, you will find tips for getting the most out of your inference lesson in the classroom.

Introducing Inference to Your Students

Making the process of inference concrete for students can be a challenge, but there are many good (and fun) ways to do it. Here are four ideas.

1. Make it visual. A simple sequence organizer can help students internalize the steps in making an inference. For example:

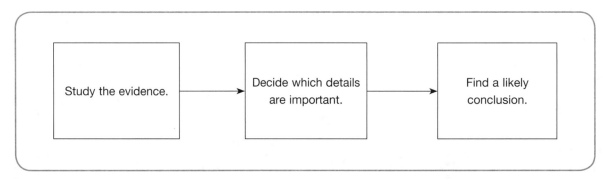

Once students understand the process on paper, model it by showing them how you work through these three steps. Short texts like poems and fables are ideal for modeling inference, but don't be afraid to use other kinds of information sources like jokes, statements, or video clips (see numbers 2–4 below).

2. Use jokes and cartoons. We don't need research to tell us that humor in the classroom is a great way to engage students. But the research is there, nonetheless. In *Laughing and Learning*, Peter Jonas (2010) surveyed the research on humor in the classroom and found that the effective use of humor increases student productivity, improves learning, and leads to better, more memorable instruction. What better way, then, to teach students about inference than through jokes and cartoons? Luckily for us, many jokes rely on inference. Here's an example:

> A man tells his doctor that he's worried about his wife's hearing. The doctor tells him to try this simple test: stand 20 feet away and ask her a question. Do the same from 10 feet, and then a third time right behind her.
>
> When the man gets home, his wife is at the stove. He stands 20 feet away and asks, "What's for dinner?"
>
> No answer.
>
> He tries again from 10 feet. "What's for dinner?"
>
> Again, nothing.

Finally, from just a foot behind her, he asks, "What's for dinner?"

His wife turns around and says, "For the third time—salmon!"

Here's another:

Jim: Hey, Joe. I'm calling you from my car. I'm on Route 715.

Joe: Route 715? Be careful, Jim! They just said on the news that a madman is driving the wrong way on 715!

Jim: One madman? Are you kidding me? There must be hundreds of them!

Jokes like these can help students see what makes an inference an inference. Ask students what's happening in the joke and what makes it funny. Then ask them whether the joke explicitly states that the husband is the one with the hearing problem or that Jim is the wrong-way driver. How did they figure it out if the joke never stated it? The answers students give are the inferences they made.

In addition to jokes, cartoons like *The Far Side* or those found in *The New Yorker* (www.newyorker cartoons.com) can also be used to isolate the process of inference.

3. Use statements. Remember those iridium statements from Section 1 (p. 3)? We bring them up again because they can really help you isolate and teach inference. Take a look at them. How might you design a similar set of statements for your subject or grade level?

4. Use pop culture. Inference-making is everywhere in the movies and on television, especially in the legal and crime genres, where lawyers and detectives piece together clues to draw conclusions. One of our favorite depictions of the power of inference is found in the comedy *My Cousin Vinny*, when Joe Pesci's character puts his fiancée, played by Marisa Tomei, on the stand. After looking at a picture of tire tracks, Tomei's character is able to make a series of inferences that establish the defendants' innocence. Unrealistic? Probably. A highly enjoyable scene? Absolutely. Inference made clear? Without question.

Emphasize the Importance of Evidence

A second concept that's crucial to all inference strategies and that warrants classroom discussion is *evidence*. What is evidence? When, where, and how is evidence used in the world? What does evidence do? Whenever students make inferences, remind them that not all inferences are created equal and that the best inferences are made on the basis of evidence. Use the inferences students make as opportunities to explore the evidence behind the inferences. And when using an inference strategy, help students go beyond finding a likely conclusion by asking questions like

- Is there any evidence that runs counter to the inference or conclusion?
- Can the same pieces of evidence support a different conclusion?
- Do you need to rethink your conclusion on the basis of the evidence?

To help students internalize this final step in making an inference, we can add a fourth box to our simple sequence organizer to represent the process of testing and refining conclusions and hypotheses in light of new evidence:

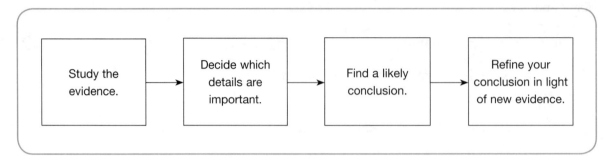

Finally, keep in mind that every inference strategy offers a perfect opportunity to conduct formative assessment. While students are working and thinking, move around the room. Pay attention to when and where they get stuck and to the confusion they articulate or demonstrate in their work. There are never enough opportunities to see, in real time, how well students are thinking inferentially, so use the ones that these strategies afford you.

Strategy-Specific Tips

Now let's look at a few tips we've learned from both researchers and teachers over the years on how to ensure effective implementation of each of the four inference strategies discussed in this PLC Guide.

Tips for Using Inductive Learning

Tip 1: Get the most out of the items students will be grouping. Inductive Learning works best when you want students to make connections among the specific elements of the content to form generalizations. When selecting items for students to group, use these general guidelines:

- Select between 12 and 40 terms, depending on your objectives and grade level.
- Make sure items are specific, not general. The idea here is to discover the general *through* the specific. If you want students to discover that farming was important to the Ancient Egyptians, for example, include specific words like *crops, planting,* and *harvest,* not general ones like *farming* or *agriculture.*
- You need at least two (preferably three or more) items to represent each concept. Otherwise, no grouping is possible.
- Even if you are using Inductive Learning to introduce new content, select a majority (about 75 percent) of items that are already familiar to students. Use the remaining 25 percent to introduce new vocabulary terms or concepts. Allow students to look up any unfamiliar words before and during the grouping process. That way, students connect new terms to familiar ones and put them into larger categories, deepening their connection to the new terms and facilitating recall.
- Don't limit yourself to words or phrases. You can develop great Inductive Learning lessons that challenge students to group quotations, mathematical expressions, physical objects, musical

instruments, pictures, lines of poetry, or anything else that lends itself to categorization according to common attributes.

- Remind students that they are free to place the same item in multiple groups.

Tip 2: Model both obvious and creative groupings. When you use Inductive Learning for the first time, you'll need to model the grouping-and-labeling process for students. When modeling this process, start with obvious groups, but encourage students to think outside the box as well by modeling groups that make more subtle connections. Figure 2.14 shows an obvious and a subtle grouping.

Figure 2.14 Obvious Versus Subtle Grouping

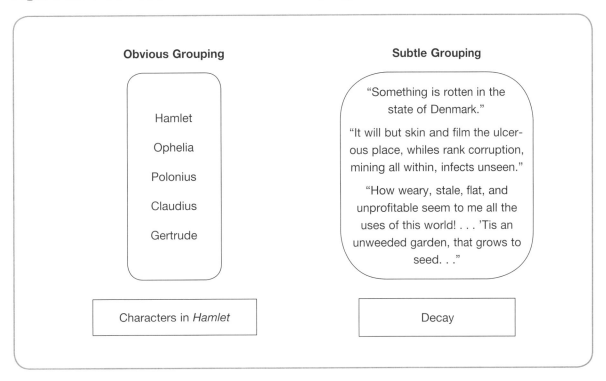

Tip 3: Use "stretching" questions. Be prepared to help students move beyond the obvious when they group the items into categories. When students reach a standstill, or when they miss subtle relationships among items, use questions like these to help them go deeper:

- What other items might go in that group?
- Can you come up with a more descriptive label for that group?
- If you added this item to your group, would the label still work? If not, how would you rename the group?
- Can you break that group into two groups?
- Can you put those two groups into a larger group?
- What if you took this item out of the group? Would that change anything?
- Why does this item belong in this group?

Tips for Using Mystery

Tip 1: Play up the intrigue. Of all the inference strategies, Mystery is the one that capitalizes most on creating a strong and compelling sense of intrigue. Take advantage of the curiosity-piquing power of this strategy by taking the time to set up the lesson as a mystery to be solved, an unusual phenomenon to be explained, or a secret to be revealed. For example,

- If the Civil War was such a mismatch on paper, why did it last for more than four years?
- Why did the Neanderthals disappear while *Homo sapiens* went on to cover the globe?
- How do great writers get us to see images in our minds using only words?
- What's happening to the honeybees? Why are they disappearing at such an alarming rate?

If possible, get students to "experience" the mystery through visualization. Ask them to close their eyes and imagine life as a Neanderthal, for example, on the verge of starvation, tracking animals through the wild in a desperate hunt for food.

Tip 2: Be a mystery detective. Be on the lookout for articles and books that use the "Three *E*s" to explain mysteries: event, evidence, explanation. (This is a more common genre than you might expect, with books like *How Come? Every Kid's Science Questions Explained* [Wollard & Solomon, 1993], *TIME for Kids Big Book of Why* [Time for Kids, 2010], and *The Book of Why* [Laffon, de Chabaneix, & Azam, 2006].) Texts like these make it easy to set up Mystery lessons. Supply students with the *event*, present the *evidence* as clues, and suppress the *explanation*.

Tip 3: Ask students to generate tentative hypotheses up front. Before students examine a single clue, ask them to go out on a cognitive limb by generating a tentative hypothesis. Why? Two reasons: first, with a tentative hypothesis in hand, students approach the clues with greater focus. Second, a tentative hypothesis that is the student's own increases engagement, as the student sets out to test and explore his or her own idea rather than a ready-made or teacher-generated one.

To facilitate this process, allow students to brainstorm everything they know about the topic of the mystery (e.g., What do you know about the Civil War? What do you know about the North and the South?). Then encourage students to use their prior knowledge to generate their best hypothesis.

Tip 4: Make your clues "clue-y." The best clues

- Are concise.
- Are groupable (i.e., they go together with other clues to form clue groups).
- Contain highly relevant information.

Added points for

- Using authentic clues (e.g., excerpts from primary documents).
- Mixing in visual, data-based, and multimedia clues.

Tips for Using Main Idea

Tip 1: Teach students how to look for cues in the text. Proficient readers are adept at separating essential from nonessential textual information, in part because they know how to pick up cues from the texts they read. These cues (adapted from van Dijk & Kintsch, 1983) include

- *Print cues*: italic, boldface, and highlighted type.
- *Word cues*: words like *key, important, significant,* and *critical,* which call attention to essential information.
- *Sentence cues*: sentences (or paragraphs) that summarize previous information or preview upcoming information, indicating that the information is especially noteworthy.
- *Organization cues*: standard prose structures like sequence, description, and cause and effect, which reveal the larger pattern of the information.

Central to the Main Idea strategy—and to good reading in general—is the ability to use these cues to make decisions about the importance of particular information. Teach students how to find and use these cues when they're looking for "feel-important" words and when they're assembling their evidence in support of their Main Idea.

Tip 2: Keep it simple. Although we always recommend using the posters included with our PLC Guides to help students understand their roles in a given strategy, the INFER acronym used in this guide's poster may be confusing to students who are being introduced to the Main Idea strategy. For this reason, we recommend creating a simpler poster that looks like this:

Figure 2.15 Main Idea Poster

*I***dentify** the topic, of the reading and words and phrases that seem especially important.

D*etermine* what the reading is saying about the topic, using one sentence. This sentence is your main idea.

E*stablish* which details in the text support the main idea.

A*sk* yourself, "Do all of the details support my main idea?" If not, consider rewriting your main idea so that all of the details support it.

Tips for Using Investigation

Tip 1: Know your frameworks. Investigation is the most open-ended of all the inference strategies, lending itself to a variety of frameworks and formats for classroom use. In this PLC Guide, we have presented a number of possible frameworks for Investigation, but by no means are these all of them. As you use Investigation regularly, try using any one of the "Puzzles to Paradoxes" frameworks shown in Figure 2.16 (pp. 78–81), which are adapted from *Tools for Thoughtful Assessment* (Boutz, Silver, Jackson, & Perini, 2012).

Figure 2.16 "Puzzles to Paradoxes" Frameworks

Framework	How to Create One	Classroom Examples
Puzzles require students to examine parts of or phases in a process or system and fit them together into a meaningful whole.	1. Break down a process, system, or text into parts. 2. Present the parts to students. 3. Challenge students to reconstruct the original and explain the logic behind the reconstruction.	• Putting the phases of the digestive process in order and explaining the sequence. • Using context, rhyme scheme, and understanding of punctuation and grammar to reconstruct a famous poem whose lines have been scrambled. • Assembling a scrambled geometric proof. • Rebuilding an engine.
Historical investigations ask students to research historical events, explore cause-and-effect relationships, and draw conclusions.	1. Choose a historically significant event. 2. Pose a question that asks students to think analytically about the causes and/or effects of the event. 3. Ask students to conduct research and present their analysis in writing.	• Why do athletes from around the world compete in the Olympics every four years? How did this tradition get started? Why do the Olympics still matter today? • What is the Treaty of Versailles? Why was it enacted? Did it have an overall positive or negative effect on Europe? • Do any passages from FDR's 1936 "A Rendezvous with Destiny" speech ring true today? Explain your answer using specific examples.

Figure 2.16 "Puzzles to Paradoxes" Frameworks (*continued*)

Framework	How to Create One	Classroom Examples
Controversies ask students to take and defend positions on unsettled or unresolved issues within the disciplines.	1. Identify a question or issue that experts have different theories about. 2. Challenge students to research the issue, take a position, and justify that position using evidence. 3. Encourage students to respond to counterarguments.	• Do we really need dangerous animals like scorpions and snakes? Wouldn't we be better off without them? • What's the value of homework? • What is the best way to stimulate the economy during a recession? • Do street artists deserve to be studied alongside art giants like Picasso and Matisse?
Moral/ethical dilemmas are similar to controversies but place more emphasis on students' personal values and judgments.	1. Identify a morally charged issue that students are likely to have different beliefs about. 2. Pose a question that requires students to take a position. 3. Have students present and defend their ideas in writing. 4. Encourage students to present the positive and negative consequences of their positions.	• Is breaking the law ever justified? • Should animals be used for scientific research? • Should our constitutionally given right to free speech be limited under any circumstances?
Paradoxes present seemingly contradictory data or situations and ask students to generate possible explanations.	1. Present students with a paradoxical statement. 2. Challenge students to reconcile the paradox by generating explanations.	How is it possible that . . . • Removing a predator from an ecosystem can actually *decrease* the number of prey? • Burning a forest can be good for its health? • Eating fewer calories can lead to weight gain? • Native Americans were already here, but people say that Columbus discovered America?

Figure 2.16 "Puzzles to Paradoxes" Frameworks (*continued*)

Framework	How to Create One	Classroom Examples
Problem-solving frameworks ask students to analyze a problem and propose a solution (or evaluate someone else's solution).	1. Present a problem that could be addressed in various ways. 2. Have students generate and present an original solution (or evaluate someone else's solution).	• How can we get people to care more about recycling? • Develop a strategy for keeping students alert and attentive during classroom lectures. • How has the "cat program" at Indiana State Prison affected inmates and corrections officers? Can you propose another program that might have similar effects? Explain and defend your plan.
Inventions challenge students to create a product that solves a problem or addresses a need.	1. Challenge students to identify a problem, a need, or a flaw in a current product. 2. Encourage students to invent something that addresses the problem, need, or flaw.	• The local zoo has hired you to redesign the enclosure for an animal of your choice. The new enclosure should promote the health and happiness of your animal while providing maximum visibility and entertainment for zoo visitors. • Invent a fitness routine that people could do in their hotel rooms without any special equipment.
Decision-making frameworks require students to consider alternatives and make decisions (or evaluate others' decisions).	1. Pose a question that asks students to consider alternatives and make a decision. 2. Have students present and explain their decision in writing (or evaluate someone else's decision).	• Imagine people from another planet who don't know what *friendship* is. Which book from our unit would you pick to help them understand what friendship means? Why? • If you had $10,000 to invest, which investment strategy would be the best choice? • Who was the most influential Transcendentalist author?

Figure 2.16 "Puzzles to Paradoxes" Frameworks (*continued*)

Framework	How to Create One	Classroom Examples
Informed predictions present students with "What if?" scenarios and ask them to generate possible outcomes.	1. Present a "What if?" scenario. 2. Ask students to speculate on possible outcomes, reminding them that predicting should be rooted in logic and knowledge (i.e., not nonsensical).	• What if Thomas Edison had never lived? • What if there were no plants? • What if Harriet Beecher Stowe had never written *Uncle Tom's Cabin?* • What if there were no oil in the Middle East?
Essential attributes ask students to define or recognize critical attributes of important concepts or apply concepts in ways that demonstrate deep understanding.	1. Select a topic central to what students are learning. 2. Test students' understanding of this concept with a task that requires mastery of the concept's essential attributes.	• Show that you understand the key elements of a fable by writing and illustrating one of your own. • Is Arthur Miller's Willy Loman a true tragic hero? Defend your position in a short essay. • Which of these pieces best represents the Baroque style of music? Why?
Experimental inquiries challenge students to generate original hypotheses and then test those hypotheses.	1. Ask students to make a hypothesis about the outcome of an action, event, or experiment. 2. Challenge students to design a plan for testing their hypotheses. 3. Whenever possible, have students carry out their plans and report on the results.	• If you were a plant, do you think the kind of light you got would matter (e.g., artificial light versus sunlight)? How would you test your predictions? • How might fewer lectures and more hands-on activities affect learning and motivation? Make a prediction and explain how we could test it as a class.

Source: Adapted from *Tools for Thoughtful Assessment,* by A. L. Boutz, H. F. Silver, J. W. Jackson, and M. J. Perini, 2012, Ho-Ho-Kus, NJ: Thoughtful Education Press. © 2012 Silver Strong & Associates/Thoughtful Education Press. Used with permission.

ThoughtWork

Before the Next Section

Between this section and the next, you will be teaching your inference lesson in your own classroom. Use the questions below to help you identify problems you might encounter as you use inference in your classroom and to develop solutions to potential problems before they actually occur.

Activity: Rooting Out Problems

1. What types of problems might you encounter while teaching an inference lesson?

2. What patterns do you see as you think about these potential problems?

3. Select one type of problem. What are the facts you know about this problem?

4. What are some possible causes for this type of problem?

5. What is the best solution to this problem?

ThoughtWork

When it comes to improving the quality of instruction, there are few resources more valuable than a critical friend who listens to your thinking, observes your work, and offers constructive feedback to help you get better results in the classroom. That's why we strongly recommend that you select a critical friend and schedule time to observe each other in the classroom. The two of you should take turns: you present your lesson to your class while your partner takes notes. Then switch roles. Use the following observation guide to structure your observation notes. When you start Section 3, be prepared to share what you have learned as a result of implementing and observing an inference lesson.

Inference Observation Guide

Which inference strategy did the teacher use?

Inductive Learning ☐   Mystery ☐   Main Idea ☐   Investigation ☐

Phase One: *Identify* What You Need to Figure Out

1. How did the teacher pique students' interest?

2. How well did the students understand the strategy and their roles in it?

ThoughtWork

Phase Two: *Note* Information Sources and Look for Patterns

1. What information sources did students use?

2. How did students interact with the information?

3. What kind of visual organizer did the teacher use? Did students understand how to use it?

ThoughtWork

Phase Three: *Formulate and Refine Hypotheses*

1. How did the teacher help students establish tentative hypotheses?

2. How well did students gather relevant evidence? How open were they to refining their hypotheses?

ThoughtWork

Phase Four: *E*xplain Your Thinking

1. How well did students discuss their thinking and evidence?

2. How did the teacher extend discussion and encourage students to elaborate on their thinking?

3. What task did the teacher assign to help students synthesize their learning?

Phase Five: *R*eflect on the Process

1. How did the teacher encourage students to reflect on the content and the process?

Evaluating the Lesson

The goal in this section is to deepen your understanding of inference strategies by working in teams to reflect on and refine your practice.

In this section you will

- Share your experiences implementing and observing an inference lesson in the classroom.

- Reflect more deeply on your own lesson by exploring specific questions about its implementation and effectiveness.

Sharing Your Experience

Now that you have conducted a lesson using an inference strategy and observed one of your peers doing the same, it's time to share what you have learned with your learning club. We recommend following the steps below:

Step 1: Using the observation guide provided in Section 2 (pp. 83–86), present your observations of *your partner's* lesson to the group.

Step 2: When you are finished, your partner will use the questions below to comment on the challenges and successes that he or she experienced while presenting the lesson.

Step 3: Next, switch roles so that your partner can present his or her observations of *your* lessons.

Step 4: Now it's your turn to share the challenges and successes you experienced during your own lesson.

Activity: Reflecting on Your Inference Lesson

1. **What goal(s) did you set out to achieve?**

2. **What steps did you take? What was hard for you?**

3. **What came naturally?**

4. **What worked about the lesson, and what just wouldn't work?**

After the presentations to the group, meet again with your partner to discuss the notes you both made. What stood out in your partner's lesson? What questions did the lesson raise for you about the strategy? How might you improve on your partner's lesson or on the process of implementing inference strategies in general?

Now consider the feedback your partner gave you. Use the space below to expand on your partner's ideas for how to improve your lesson. Include what you thought you did well, how your students responded to the lesson, what aspects of the process worked best for you, and what you might do differently next time.

Activity: Improving Your Use of Inference Strategies

How might you improve your next lesson? How might you improve your implementation of inference strategies?

For the ThoughtWork activity on the next page, you will design another inference lesson for your classroom. You may choose to begin planning now as part of a learning club meeting, or you may prefer to plan on your own or with your critical friend outside the meeting.

ThoughtWork

Before the Next Section

Before the final section, complete the following exercises:

- Plan another lesson using one of the four inference strategies. Use the inference planning forms provided in Section 2 (pp. 67–71) to guide you.
- Present the lesson you designed to your students.
- Collect three samples of student work from your lesson and bring them to the next meeting. The student work you collect should reflect what you believe to be three distinct skill levels: low-level, average, and high-level. To see how one teacher selected her levels, preview pages 94–98 in Section 4.
- Bring enough copies of your student work to distribute to the members of your learning club.

Learning from Student Work

The goal in this section is to examine student work at various levels of proficiency and use it to help you refine your work in designing and delivering inference lessons.

In this section you will

■ See how a teacher selected and analyzed her three samples of student work.

■ Share and discuss the student work you collected.

■ Develop a rubric for assessing student work based on your discussion and samples.

■ Plan your next steps in building students' inference and comprehension skills.

Examining Samples

In this final section, you are going to use student work to assess the effectiveness of your instruction, your students' inference skills, and your students' grasp of the content. Let's start with a model to guide your examination of the student work you collected for this section.

Here is a Mystery lesson designed by a middle school history teacher.

Mystery Lesson: Jamestown Colony

Jamestown Colony on the Brink of Ruin!

This could easily have been a headline in the 1620s. Plymouth Colony and Jamestown were the first two settlements established by the English on the North American continent. Although neither of these colonial ventures found it easy to establish a successful and independent settlement, the Virginia colony at Jamestown was in the greatest peril. Within its first 20 years, Jamestown had a death rate that was 75–80 percent of its population! Nearly 6,000 people had immigrated to Jamestown, but by 1622 there were only 700 residents left. By this time the local Native American tribes had moved into the interior and posed little danger.

What Happened to All the People?

As a student of history, you have been asked to join a historical study team to determine just what conditions would result in such a large drop in population. Your challenge is to examine the clues provided and construct a theory that explains what happened in Jamestown.

Specifically, your mission is to answer these questions:

- What was going on in the colony at the time?
- What was the cause of the excessive death rate?
- Who was dying?
- Why did the high death rate last for so long?

To synthesize their learning, students were asked to write an essay explaining the mystery surrounding the unusually high death rate in the Jamestown colony. Let's look at three students' essays at three levels of proficiency: low, average, and high.

Example of Low-Level Student Work: Jacob's Essay

Jamestown

Life in Jamestown was tough. People were dying left and right. Everyone was so busy trying to make tobacco. They forgot to do all of the other things. They even forgot to make food like corn.

The reason was tobacco. It took too much work to grow it. But the colonists kept trying anyway. One clue said it was worth even more money than gold. Nowadays tobacco is expensive, but it's not worth as much as gold.

Example of Average Student Work: Marissa's Essay

Life in Jamestown

In Jamestown, tobacco was the most important thing. It was so important to the colonists that they let almost everything else go.

Tobacco was everywhere. All the available farmland was used to grow it. They stored it in churches. Colonists didn't bother to take care of their homes because they were so busy planting tobacco. It got so bad that the government had to start passing laws to try to get people to grow corn. But it didn't matter. They just kept growing tobacco.

Tobacco was worth lots of money. So that's why the colonists didn't listen to the government and start planting corn. With nobody growing any food, people started starving. People got sick and no one cared because the colonists just kept working on growing more tobacco. More and more people kept coming to try to get rich by tobacco. But there was no food and typhoid fever was spreading and crime started getting bad. That's how almost 80 percent of the people died in Jamestown.

The Mystery of Jamestown's Vanishing Population

In the Jamestown colony in Virginia, death was everywhere. Between 1607 and 1622, an astounding 80 percent of the original population disappeared. Why was it so hard to survive in Jamestown? Because in Jamestown, profits were more important than people.

The economy of Jamestown was focused entirely on tobacco. From 1613 to 1618, tobacco exports increased from 200 to over 49,000 pounds per year, which shows how focused people were on making a profit on this crop. Tobacco was a difficult crop to harvest and it took up most of the workers' time. The corn crops became so neglected that the government instituted a law in 1618 insisting that each man plant corn or he would be strongly fined. The law got stricter each year.

Because the colonists were so focused on growing tobacco, the Jamestown colony fell apart. Nearly every square inch of land was being used for planting tobacco. People spent most of their time working on the tobacco crops. Virginia was an extremely unhealthy place to live. People were getting typhoid fever from contaminated wells, animals were disappearing, and houses were not maintained. Even the churches were used for tobacco storage. Finally, Virginia became ungovernable and crime worsened.

So why did people keep coming to Jamestown? Well, the people who came from England when conditions were already bad in Jamestown were described in an excerpt from an old newspaper as "slum dwellers, convicts, and poor farmers." They must have been very desperate people who had very little chance of succeeding in England. For those who were desperate, the idea of getting rich by growing tobacco must have been so powerful that they were willing to risk their lives by coming to one of the most dangerous places imaginable. For the poor, as well as for almost everyone else in Jamestown, the chance to make a profit came first.

Take a moment to examine your thinking about the student work samples you have just reviewed. What do you notice about the high-level sample that is missing from the other two? Which criteria might you use to compare these levels, and how might you describe each sample based on those criteria? Record your thoughts in the space below.

Activity: Reflecting on Sample Student Work

Possible criteria:

The teacher who developed the essay task on the mystery of Jamestown created the rubric in Figure 4.1 to guide her assessment of student work. You may want to use this rubric as a model when you develop your own rubric later in this section.

Figure 4.1 Teacher's Rubric for Essay Task: The Mystery of Jamestown

	High-Level Performance	Average Performance	Low-Level or Struggling Performance
Content	• Essay includes all relevant information from the lesson. • Essay recognizes relationships found in the information. • Essay fully recognizes and elaborates on key ideas. • The writing is relevant and focused on the topic.	• Essay includes some relevant information but may show some misunderstanding. • Essay shows partial recognition of relationships found in the information. • Essay shows general recognition of key ideas. • The writing is focused on the topic for most of the piece.	• Essay is missing relevant information. • Essay shows limited recognition of relationships found in the information. • Essay shows limited recognition of key ideas. • The writing lacks focus.
Process	• The hypothesis is clearly stated at or near the beginning of the essay. • The writing includes specific evidence that supports the hypothesis. • The writing foresees and addresses possible counterarguments.	• The hypothesis is stated. • The writing includes some supporting evidence. • The writing shows only partial recognition of counterarguments.	• The hypothesis is unclear. • The writing provides little supporting evidence. • The writing shows no recognition of counterarguments.
Product	• Ideas are fully developed. • Essay has a strong sense of "flow": ideas are organized and transitions are used. • Essay is highly persuasive. • Essay follows writing conventions appropriately.	• Some ideas are developed. • Essay is organized around key ideas; some transitions are missing or weak. • Essay is somewhat persuasive. • Essay follows most writing conventions.	• Ideas lack development. • Essay shows minimal organization. • Essay is unpersuasive. • Essay shows limited understanding of writing conventions.

Let's now turn to your thought process in selecting your own student work samples. Take a few minutes to reexamine your samples, keeping in mind the following questions:

- How did you select work from each level?
- Which criteria did you use to choose this work?

Record your thoughts in the space provided below.

Activity: How You Selected Student Work Samples

Level One: High-Level

Level Two: Average

Level Three: Low-Level or Struggling

Next, meet with your partner to share the student work you collected. Work together to analyze the content, process, and product of the student work. Keep in mind that examining this student work is less about whether commas and semicolons are in the right place and more about how well students have applied their understanding of the content and the power of inferential thinking.

Note that we have provided two different formats for this collaborative analysis. Option 1 (p. 100) uses questions to guide the analysis. Option 2 (p. 101) uses a rubric format. Decide which option works better for you and your partner and use it to conduct your analysis.

Activity: Analyzing Student Work, Option 1—Questions

Content

1. What does the student work suggest about students' grasp of the key ideas and details?

2. Which parts of the content are firmly in their grasp?

3. Which ideas and details are slipping through the cracks?

Process

1. What does this work suggest about your students' abilities to make inferences, draw conclusions, and justify their reasoning?

Product

1. What similarities and differences do you notice in the quality of student work?

2. How well are students communicating their ideas?

3. What signs are there that students are reaching toward excellence? What patterns of strength and weakness do you find compelling?

Activity: Analyzing Student Work, Option 2—Rubric

	High-Level Performance	Average Performance	Low-Level or Struggling Performance
Content			
Process			
Product			

Now, summarize what you have learned from your analysis and plan your next steps.

Activity: Thinking About the Next Steps

Content

What have you learned about your students' grasp of ideas and details in the content area?

Process

What have you learned about your students' ability to make inferences and explain their reasoning?

Product

What have you learned about your students' ability to communicate? What motivates them to reach toward excellence?

Interventions

How will you use these insights? What kinds of instructional interventions do you need to make?*

*For a collection of ready-to-use instructional techniques for helping students meet your benchmarks, see *Tools for Promoting Active, In-Depth Learning* (Silver, Strong, & Perini, 2001).

Where Am I Now?

Before completing this guide, take a few minutes to think about your own grasp of the inference strategies in this guide. Look at the strategy implementation milestones below. Where do you think you are now? What do you need to do to move to the next level?

Strategy Implementation Milestones

I am familiar with inference strategies and can describe what they look like in the classroom.

✓ I understand and can explain how these strategies work.

✓ I have planned several inference lessons, used them in my classroom, and reflected with my colleagues on their effects on my students.

✓ My students have a solid understanding of how to use inference strategies on their own, and I can see them transferring the thinking skills involved in these strategies to other situations.

✓ I am ready to teach other people how to use inference strategies.

Appendix A: Inductive Writing: Learning Takes a "Write" Turn

At the heart of the Inductive Learning strategy is a grouping-and-labeling process that, once completed, suggests a larger organizational structure. This same process can be put to great effect when helping students write multi-paragraph essays. We call this writing-based variation *Inductive Writing*. Inductive Writing's emphasis on assembling details, identifying the big ideas that unite those details, and organizing information into a meaningful structure corresponds directly to the challenges many students face when asked to write constructed-response or open-ended essays.

Here's how to implement Inductive Writing in your classroom.

1. Help students generate ideas related to the topic. Carly Duhaime's middle school students are working on developing personal narratives that relate a time when they experienced overwhelming fear. After students have selected their incidents, Carly helps them generate rich associations by asking them to close their eyes and dig deep into their memories. As students recall their incidents, Carly poses questions: What do you see? What do you hear? What do you smell? What emotions are you experiencing? What are you thinking during this incident? (Note that different types of writing call for different kinds of questions. For example, if a teacher wanted students to write an informative essay based on a topic they had learned about, questions would likely be geared toward helping students get all of their background knowledge out into the open. And explanatory essays would call for more "how" and "why" questions.)

During and after this thinking activity, students write down words, phrases, snippets of dialogue, images, feelings, and memories that come to mind. A student named Ally generated the following list.

Six Flags	roller coaster	hearing people scream
"I can do it! I can do it!"	massive	steel
heart racing	dizzy	nauseous
squeezing the restraints hard	shooting up the tower	waiting in line forever
Kingda Ka	tallest coaster in the world	400-foot drop
towering	falling from the sky	coming to a stop
my dad asked me if I was OK	my brother making fun of me	
I pretended I wasn't scared	That was it?	

2. Have students group and label their associations into related categories. Carly asks students to look over their lists and to think about how they might use their associations to plan out their essay. Specifically, she asks students to

- Place associations that seem to go together into groups.
- Imagine that each group will serve as the basis for a paragraph.
- Create a topic sentence for each group that tells what the paragraph will be about.
- Sequence the groups into an order that makes sense.

As students develop their groups and labels, Carly moves around the room to assess students' abilities to create meaningful groups, develop topic sentences, and think through a writing sequence. Carly works with students who are struggling and encourages all students to add to and revise their lists to make more cohesive groups.

After reviewing and modifying her associations, Ally created the groups shown in Figure A.1.

Figure A.1 Ally's Groups for Inductive Writing

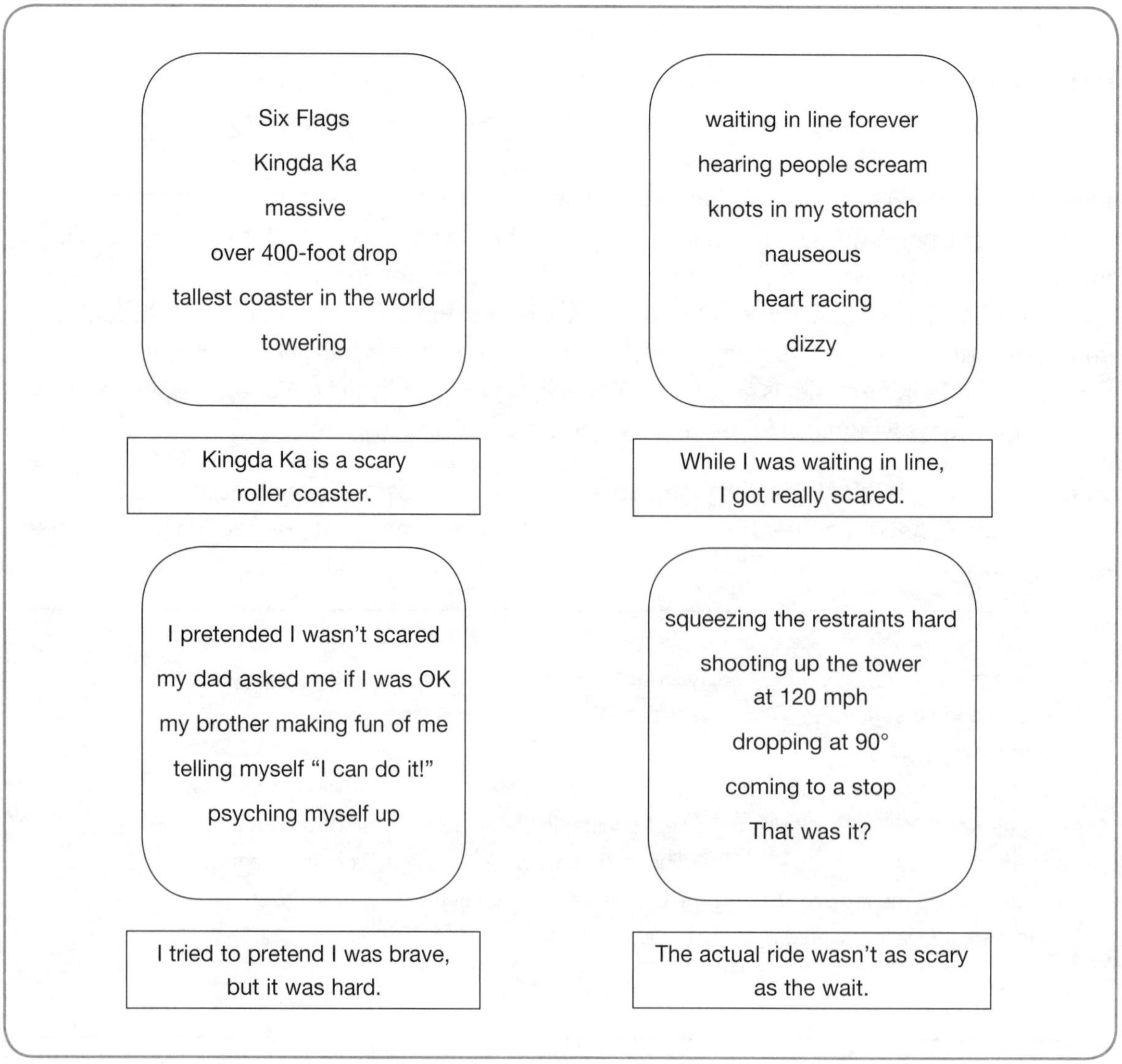

3. Ask students to produce a first draft. Before students begin writing, Carly asks them to consider these questions:

- Are your groups complete? Are there any important details that you might be missing?
- Are your topic sentences supported? Do all the details in each group support the topic sentence? Do you need to revise any topic sentences to be clearer or more accurate?
- Can you think your way through the essay? Do you feel the flow? Can you envision how each paragraph will lead to the next? Do you know how it will open and close?

Students then draft their essays individually.

4. Provide opportunities for students to refine their work. Students work in Writer's Clubs to read one another's writing and provide feedback and suggestions for how to improve it. After meeting with her Writer's Club, Ally realized she could make her writing more engaging by incorporating some dialogue and refining her opening sentence and her conclusion. Ally's revised personal narrative appears in Figure A.2.

Figure A.2 Ally's Revised Personal Narrative

Kingda Ka isn't just any ordinary roller coaster. It's the biggest, most terrifying roller coaster in the world. When I arrived at Six Flags with my family, it was the first thing I saw. How could anyone miss it? It has a massive 400-foot drop that towers over the whole park. My father, mother, and little brother, Tommy, were all excited to go on Kingda Ka. I thought I was too, but once I saw how high it was, I wasn't so sure.

While we were waiting in line, all I could hear were the people screaming. It sounded like they were afraid for their lives. Suddenly, I felt dizzy. I had knots in my stomach. My hands were trembling, my heart was racing, and I felt nauseous.

I had to pretend I was OK or Tommy would never let me live it down. I tried to smile and to have a normal conversation. But I wasn't doing such a good job.

"Are you OK, Ally?" my father asked.

I lied and said I was fine.

"Maybe you should just stick to kiddie rides," my brother teased me.

I ignored him. In my head, I was trying to psych myself up by saying, "I can do this! I can do this!" over and over again.

Figure A.2 Ally's Revised Personal Narrative (*continued*)

Finally, it was time to ride. I was still talking to myself in my head when the restraints went down over me. I squeezed the restraints hard and then—AAAAH! We were shooting forward at 120 miles per hour. We were flying up the tower, until we weren't anymore. And then we were falling, falling, falling, straight down at 90°. And you know what? I wasn't scared anymore. I was excited. I was brave. I was having fun!

When we came to a stop, my brother looked over at me, expecting me to be crying or to throw up. Instead I shrugged my shoulders and said, "That was it?"

5. Encourage students to reflect on the process. To help students generalize some of the skills they've learned, Carly conducts a discussion guided by these questions:

- What did you learn about how to organize your ideas?
- How did working in your Writer's Club help you improve your writing?
- How might you use this technique for other kinds of writing tasks and assignments?

Appendix B: What Are the Habits of Mind?

Habits of mind are dispositions that are skillfully and mindfully employed by characteristically intelligent, successful people when they are confronted with problems whose solutions are not immediately apparent.

The habits of mind as identified by Art Costa and Bena Kallick (2008, 2009) are

- Persisting.
- Thinking and communicating with clarity and precision.
- Managing impulsivity.
- Gathering data through all senses.
- Listening with understanding and empathy.
- Creating, imagining, and innovating.
- Thinking flexibly.
- Responding with wonderment and awe.
- Thinking about thinking (metacognition).
- Taking responsible risks.
- Striving for accuracy.
- Finding humor.
- Questioning and posing problems.
- Thinking interdependently.
- Applying past knowledge to new situations.
- Remaining open to continuous learning.

To learn more about the habits of mind and how schools across the globe are using them to improve teaching and learning, go to www.instituteforhabitsofmind.com.

References

Boutz, A. L., Silver, H. F., Jackson, J. W., & Perini, M. J. (2012). *Tools for thoughtful assessment.* Ho-Ho-Kus, NJ: Thoughtful Education Press.

Costa, A. L., & Kallick, B. (Eds.). (2008). *Learning and leading with habits of mind: 16 essential characteristics for success.* Alexandria, VA: ASCD.

Costa, A. L., & Kallick, B. (2009). *Habits of mind across the curriculum: Practical and creative strategies for teachers.* Alexandria, VA: ASCD.

Dickinson, E. (1961). Faith is a fine invention. In T. H. Johnson (Ed.), *Final harvest: Emily Dickinson's poems* (p. 20). Boston: Little, Brown and Company.

Hynes, M. C. (Ed.). (2004). *IDEAS: NCTM standards-based instruction, grades 5–8.* Reston, VA: National Council of Teachers of Mathematics.

Jonas, P. M. (2010). *Laughing and learning: An alternative to shut up and listen.* Lanham, MD: Rowman & Littlefield Education.

Joyce, B. R., & Showers, B. (2002). *Student achievement through staff development* (3rd ed.). Alexandria, VA: ASCD.

Laffon, M., de Chabaneix, H., & Azam, J. (2006). *The book of why.* New York: Abrams.

Marzano, R. J. (2007). *The art and science of teaching: A comprehensive framework for effective instruction.* Alexandria, VA: ASCD.

Marzano, R. J. (2010). Reimagining school: Teaching inference. *Educational Leadership, 67*(7), 80–81.

Schmoker, M. (2005). Here and now: Improving teaching and learning. In R. DuFour, R. Eaker, & R. DuFour (Eds.), *On common ground: The power of professional learning communities* (pp. xi–xvi). Bloomington, IN: Solution Tree.

Silver, H. F., & Perini, M. J. (2010). *Classroom curriculum design: How strategic units improve instruction and engage students in meaningful learning.* Ho-Ho-Kus, NJ: Thoughtful Education Press.

Silver, H. F., Strong, R. W., & Perini, M. J. (2001). *Tools for promoting active, in-depth learning* (2nd ed.). Ho-Ho-Kus, NJ: Thoughtful Education Press.

Strong, R. W., Silver, H. F., & Perini, M. J. (2008). *Reading for academic success, grades 2–6: Differentiated strategies for struggling, average, and advanced readers.* Thousand Oaks, CA: Corwin.

Taba, H., Durkin, M. C., Fraenkel, J. R., & McNaughton, A. H. (1971). *A teacher's handbook to elementary social studies: An inductive approach* (2nd ed.). Reading, MA: Addison-Wesley.

Time for Kids. (2010). *TIME for kids big book of why: 1,001 facts kids want to know.* New York: Author.

van Dijk, T. A., & Kintsch, W. (1983). *Strategies of discourse comprehension.* New York: Academic Press.

Wollord, K., & Solomon, D. (1993). *How come? Every kid's science questions explained.* New York: Workman Publishing Company.

About the Authors

Harvey F. Silver, EdD, is president of Silver Strong & Associates and Thoughtful Education Press. He has conducted numerous workshops for school districts and state education departments throughout the United States. He was the principal consultant for the Georgia Critical Thinking Skills Program and the Kentucky Thoughtful Education Teacher Leadership Program. With the late Richard W. Strong, he developed The Thoughtful Classroom—a renowned professional development initiative dedicated to the goal of "Making Students as Important as Standards." Dr. Silver may be reached at Silver Strong & Associates, 227 First Street, Ho-Ho-Kus, NJ 07423; 1-800-962-4432 (T); hsilver@thoughtfulclassroom.com.

R. Thomas Dewing, EdD, has spent more than 35 years in public education as an elementary and middle school teacher, principal, instructional coordinator, and educator of gifted students. He has also taught education courses at National Louis University and North Central College. Tom is an experienced trainer, consultant, and presenter and has worked with numerous education organizations to create curricular teaching materials and state and national assessments. He may be reached at tdewing@thoughtfulclassroom.com.

Matthew J. Perini is director of publishing for Silver Strong & Associates and Thoughtful Education Press. He has authored more than 20 books, curriculum guides, articles, and research studies covering a wide range of educational topics, including learning styles, multiple intelligences, reading instruction, and effective teaching practices. He may be reached at mperini@thoughtfulclassroom.com.

With Richard W. Strong, Silver and Perini have collaborated on a number of best sellers in education, including *The Strategic Teacher*; *So Each May Learn: Integrating Learning Styles and Multiple Intelligences*; and *Teaching What Matters Most: Standards and Strategies for Raising Student Achievement*, all published by ASCD; and Thoughtful Education Press's *Tools for Promoting Active, In-Depth Learning*, which won a Teachers' Choice Award in 2004.